Doing Life

Doing Life

A Pragmatist Manifesto

Lee Thayer

Library of Congress Control Number: 2012902261
ISBN: Hardcover   978-1-4691-6344-4
                  Softcover   978-1-4691-6343-7
                  Ebook   978-1-4691-6345-1

This book was printed in the United States of America.

To order additional copies of this book, contact:
Xlibris Corporation
1-888-795-4274
www.Xlibris.com
Orders@Xlibris.com
104577

CONTENTS

SOME PRECURSORY NOTES

This book is about "doing" life. Not about "having" a life. Everyone "has" one of those—for whatever it may or may not be worth.

Our lives evolve out of what we do—or don't do. Biological life may be a given. But conscious life is not.

To conceive of a life—one's own or another's—requires thought. No person is born capable of conscious thought. That has to be developed over time.

Our minds emerge not in biology, but in communication. We have the kind of mind we happen to have that originates and gets reinforced in communication with others.

The much-unheeded philosopher E. M. Cioran once quipped something like "*The most important decision you will ever make in your life is who to have as parents.*" That he was unheeded would probably have been okay by him. He wanted his thoughts to take people by surprise.

He believed that philosophy was about the questions or provocations that could be raised. It was not about answers. He believed that the best handle anyone could have on "the world" was a metaphorical one. And, since all of our understanding of the world we inhabit is via metaphor (as Nietzsche said), he wanted us to learn how to think metaphorically. Not literally.

Cioran assumed his readers were smart. Otherwise, they wouldn't be trying to read his (otherwise) obfuscations. He didn't think he needed to explain that we don't choose our parents. Nor do they choose us.

If we *could* choose our parents, we wouldn't be smart enough to do it to our long-term benefit. Genetics would count—for something. But what would count for more would be social status, wealth, education, and street smarts (or wisdom).

So what he is suggesting to the careful reader is that we have to compensate for what we don't get from the parents we happen to draw. And that we have to live with, or eradicate, what they provided us that limits us or leads us astray.

In other words, what we can't get by choosing our parents we have to choose by having other "parents" along the way. Not as much as our parents probably influenced us. But other people influence us continuously, and thus the conditions of our immediate lives and our destinies. That's where our destinies get percolated, daily.

In short, the likely lesson is to beware of who you listen to. Others have their own agendas. They have their own intellectual and emotional limitations.

They seldom have *our* best interests at heart. And, even if they could figure out what our best interests might be, we might not be discriminating enough to listen to the best and ignore the rest. And even the best may not be articulate enough to move us in the direction we *ought* to go.

We all get dealt a different set of cards. We have to play the game with the cards we hold. But that doesn't mean we can't win anyway—as every world-class poker player knows.

It comes down not to the hand we were dealt, but how well we learn to play the game.

Some people think that if they had just had the right "parents"—or this or that advantage in their lives—they could do life infinitely better. But by the time you become your own parent, you no longer have *that* excuse.

And as for those other dreamt-about advantages: people win or lose every day. In the game of life, you have to make it out of the hand you hold—whether good or bad. Hoping for a better set of cards is not much of a method, once the game is on.

Poker is not life. But some people make a life out of it. You may not be holding the perfect hand. But others don't know that. Or you may be holding a terrible hand. But others don't know that.

It's not the cards you hold. It's how you play the game. Life is rarely as rational or as logical as we sometimes believe it is. It is certainly not literal. The reality that matters is the reality you create out of the raw material available to you. As you think, so shall you be.

We play out our lives from within the parameters of the *roles* we are given to play. Most people seem content to take on the roles they happen to fall into—as the role we inherit by "falling" in love. Our friends are fortuitous. To have a "friend," you have to *be* a friend. Any role makes us interdependent with others. It is the role we are playing that enables and constrains us.

A few choose the roles they need to play in order to get where they want to go. They are the weird ones. They become the primary authors of the story of their lives. They solicit others to play supporting roles, or as props.

So we are more or less in-formed by the roles we take on or fall into. We have to learn the "baby" role, with its supporting cast of characters—parents, relatives, or anyone else who admires our innocence.

Every role is a part in a story. The story may be short and incidental, as when you intuitively avoid bumping into a stranger on a crowded sidewalk. Or it may continue on for years, as in a marriage or a partnership or a friendship.

Our lives are full of events. We connect-the-dots, so to speak, and make a story out of those often unrelated events in order to make sense of our lives. We have our own unique continuity in the stories that we bring to, or manufacture, to make our lives make sense.

We make sense of where we've been, who we are, and where we're going by the kinds of stories we imagine ourselves to be in. No imagination, no real life. Poor imagination, or poor capacity for implementation = a poor, or simply wrong, life.

No one has a free hand in this. You either have to adapt a prepackaged story for your life, or compose one as best you can, given the impediments you have to live with and given the possibilities you can plausibly envision.

We try to emulate the personas we look up to, or imitate those whom we happen to know. They may not be any better at doing life than you are. But you have to have a supporting cast of characters. So you have to take what you can get. Or, you have to persuade the ones you need. There is no third option: you either take life as it comes or somehow forge it to suit your purposes.

Most people adapt by creating an inner life to which only they are privy. They can be anyone they want in their imaginations. There may be slips along the way. People who live two lives—an inner life and an outer life—may occasionally mistake the one for the other. When they do, there is embarrassment all around.

How people see you is who you are in their eyes. If how you perform your life—no matter how trivial—does not match their expectations, you will have a problem.

It may not be fatal to the relationship. But it may be. If you perform a real life outside the one you belong to with another, there may be bad consequences. An affair, for example, creates an intimacy one of the spouses cannot be witness to. There will be recriminations.

What two people espouse (pun intended), and on which their relationship hinges, can unilaterally be made fraudulent. The "sin" is not in what one or the other did, but in the maiming of the relationship.

It is the absence of transparency that provides the trust that makes the relationship possible. The more transparency there is, the less love or lust—the less falling in love—but the more trustworthy the relationship. It requires deceit to make a relationship. But at some point the relationship becomes transparent. Then deceit can damage or destroy it.

The metaphor holds for most stories that involve two or more people. We need to know the story we imagine we are in to play our role in that story.

If one changes the story unilaterally, the others will likely strike back. It may be no more than utter frustration at playing the fool in a nonexistent story. But such frustration can be furious—as can be witnessed in the film *The War of the Roses*.

"The play's the thing," as Shakespeare said and as Pirandello echoed in his work for the stage. But if one of the characters doesn't fulfill his or her role, the illusions by which they are functioning come apart. The story is either sustained by your role and others' roles, or it is not. If it is not, the story takes a radical and unpredictable turn.

Being in a bad story is better than being in an incomprehensible one. That's why we humans are so adaptable. We can put up with almost any kind of role, as long as we can connect-the-dots with a story.

We live in and by our stories. The more roles you can convincingly perform, the more stories you can cast yourself in. You have to know how to play the role to get the part. Since no role is wholly unprecedented, you have to know the script (or induce others to know your script) in order to make the story go.

In other words: If you can't be the central character in your own story, you have to be a supporting character in someone else's story—or, more typically, in a standard story provided by the canon of the culture to which you belong.

Unless you were the first man or woman, you were—like all the rest of us—born into an existing, ongoing human organization of some sort—a tribe, a clan, a society. Every sort of human group has a culture. A culture is a repository for the languages we all have to learn: the one we speak, the one that provides the do's and don'ts of social life. A culture is a human group's collective consciousness and collective conscience. Some ways of behaving are prescribed. Others are proscribed.

Every culture, and every subculture, has its norms. These are loose guides to what to think, how to feel, what to do, and how to conform in other ways. Some cultures are more permissive than others. In general, traditional cultures were more constraining than modern cultures.

To be born into an existing culture means that you are expected—by osmosis if not more directly—to adopt its mores, its folklore and its proverbs, its beliefs and disbeliefs, its moralities, and all of its sanctioned ways of thinking, being, doing, having, and saying.

People have to be endorsed by others to be validated in the roles they perform. You have to audition for the role you would perform. Your life is never solely, never exclusively, your own.

You could create a self or a persona to suit no one but yourself. But then you might get locked up as "insane." Sanity in any culture is conformity to the norms, as modern psychiatrists have been slow to acknowledge. As a culture evolves, so do people's ideas about doing life within it.

To paraphrase Samuel Butler's provocative metaphor, *People are a culture's way of perpetuating itself.* It works that way. We just don't see it that way.

You could improvise in the role(s) you perform. But you could not do so beyond what is acceptable to others. The lives we "do" have to be made of the cultural materials available. And then they have to be acceptable to the others who constitute our stakeholders—those who have a stake in how we perform our lives.

We are who we are because the others who endorse us are who *they* are. And vice versa. A celebrity is a celebrity because he or she has lots of fans. The fans are those who idolize their celebrities. Some people have power over others because those others see them as having that power.

"It takes two to tango," as the well-worn saying goes. Doing life is doing a social dance. It requires partners, endorsers, supporting actors in the story we imagine ourselves to be in. To do "being in love" has no tangible existence. It exists for us because we perform it with someone who performs it with us.

As the poet T. S. Eliot wrote in his *Four Quartets,*

> "*. . . there is only the dance.*"

Doing life is doing the social dance, which is enabled and constrained by the dance one does with oneself. It is not the dancer that excites.

It is the dance. Then we are left with William Butler Yeats' famous metaphor:

> *"O body swayed to music, O brightening glance,*
> *How can we know the dancer from the dance?"*

How, indeed? It is in doing life as we do it that we are known to ourselves, and to others. Take away the doing and there is nothing of real meaning.

It is in doing life that our lives have whatever meaning they have. As we do life, so shall we be. Being has its source in doing. We do life in order to be someone in the eyes of others. It is *how* we do life that determines who we will be—as we are refracted by those who observe us, including ourselves.

Identity—who we imagine ourselves to be—comes from auditioning for the role(s) we want or are stuck with. We could be someone other than who we are. But that would require doing life other than the way we have settled for. Habits channel us down our same rutted paths.

Change may beckon. But it hasn't much of a chance up against ingrained habits. We would have to have strikingly different habits to be someone other than who we are.

We don't know how to ask the questions that would rock us out of our comfort zones. Doing life becomes a matter of doing more or less the same things over and over again—but hoping for radically different outcomes. It doesn't work that way. If you want a different outcome, you have to perform that different outcome. If you can't do so convincingly to others and hence to yourself, you can't be someone other than who you are.

Who we are is more important to us than who we might become. It was the poet/philosopher Goethe who urged us thus:

> *You must love people not for what they are, but for what*
> *they ought to be.*

Or what they could be or should be. If you are one of those people, this applies to you. We seem to be stuck with loving ourselves as we are, all of our protestations to the contrary notwithstanding. We may not even like ourselves at times. But our imagination and our will fail us.

We grow accustomed to the face of our lover (as the popular song goes), and love flounders in the accommodation. Who we are will in almost all cases overpower any desire for change.

We wouldn't have to be stuck with who we are, as we will see clearly in this book. But that assumes that this book's readers are the ones who *should be* reading this book. As we know from the research, this is not a very tenable assumption. It's likely that every serious author is mainly preaching to the choir.

There are always those who would save us from ourselves. But we rarely like them. There is no mental slot open for their advice. We prefer the advice of those who tell us that "I'm okay, you're okay."

Where change vs. stasis are concerned, okay usually rules the day.

We live simultaneously in three worlds. We live in the biological world of our bodies and their functioning. We live in the outer world of what is going on around us in our social/economic/natural world. And we live in the world of our own mental/emotional states.

All three exercise their imperatives independently of our intentions and desires.

Until some time in the future, we are encouraged to believe, the genes you were born with are the genes you have to live with. You are compellingly entreated by commercial advertising to believe that if you use just the right cosmetics, you could indeed look like a super-model. That's not going to happen. Some people are born to be beautiful (a cultural bias in any case), and some people are born to be plain, or worse.

The perfect body doesn't exist. Cosmetic surgery and tattooing may enhance your image in the eyes of people who judge things in that way. But basically you have to do life with the body you have.

Tornados and floods kill people. So do stock market crashes. Your lover can dump you. We may be faced with the fall of our empire. None of such things as these were requested by you.

We can explain anything. Experts can predict things. But things are not obligated to be the way we explain them or predict them. Their imperatives are a function of *their* indecipherable logic, not ours.

Most of what happens in our lives we do not control. We might like to control them. A guru who tells us what to eat and how to exercise drops dead. We are not immunized by what we take to be our knowledge of the world. Our explanations do not obligate the world to be as we say it is.

We have the minds we have because they got constructed that way by others, and by our internal explanations. Our feelings come from the stories we tell one another about how people are "caused" to feel this way or that when things happen. By and large, we have the feelings we believe we are supposed to have in the story we imagine we are in.

The way out of this prison we people make for ourselves is as follows.

Two of those worlds are given. The famous biologist D'Arcy Thompson once said,

> *"Things are the way they are because they got to be that way."*

That works well for people who want to *do* life rather than to have life do them. We certainly can and have learned important lessons by examining past events. But what we cannot learn there is what we *should be* doing. Facts cannot tell us how we ought to live.

Of the three worlds, the one that is not given is how we choose to *interpret* ourselves and the other two worlds. How we interpret (or explain) things determines our personal and our collective habitat. We live life in and through our minds.

It is how we talk to ourselves that is the measure of our personal and collective history. It is how we talk to ourselves that translates what we know into what we do. It is how we talk to ourselves that configures our future. It is how we interpret things that matters.

Some consider San Francisco the most beautiful city in America. The suicide rate is the highest. People self-destruct in paradise (as our mythical stories suggest), and adapt to the filth and the stench of an inner city. How is one to explain such paradoxes?

If the ultimate reality of things is paradoxical, why should we bother to explain the paradoxes of daily life? Why should we try to predict the human future? Won't people in their inimitable ways screw up the logic by which we set it forth? Why *did* Adam and Eve get kicked out of Eden?

We learned to communicate and thus to think about things. How we do so is our destiny—personally and collectively. When people were asked, "Do you want to live in the city or in the country?" their answer was overwhelmingly, "In the country." So where do most people live? In cities.

It was the eminent mathematician and man of letters Blaise Pascal who wrote, in 1670:

> *"I have discovered that all human evil comes from this,*
> *man's being unable to sit still in a room."*

If this is so, then we are doomed. If this is so, then all utopian talk is futile. People are restive. They can't let well enough alone.

Early civilizations were truth-keepers. They assumed they had all the truth they needed, and thus (as the American Indian did) dedicated their lives to other pursuits, like beauty.

Western civilization is truth-*seeking*. We believe that "the best is yet to come." The growth of what we deem to be knowledge grows as limitlessly as we say the universe does. Progress everywhere (especially in our technologies) outpaces us. How can we live "happily ever after" when any way of living is provisional and somehow inadequate? We are not thankful for what we have. We are demanding of what we don't have.

"We are, perhaps, uniquely among the earth's creatures, the worrying animal. We worry away our lives, fearing the future, discontent with the present, unable to sit still,"

That's the science writer Lewis Thomas, in *The Medusa and the Snail* (1979). Not much has changed. If we anchor our lives in discontent, with what will we be content?

We are happy only when we escape our mundane lives (as the longshoreman-turned-philosopher Eric Hoffer reminded us. We don't know how to construct joy. It comes upon us like a headache. We laugh nervously unless the laugh-track is there to prompt us. Beauty is defined by the fashion magazines. Shopping and doctoring are our two most prominent activities.

Is something seriously amiss?

Our own lives are increasingly mediated for us. We have to buy something to have a life—some magazine, some advice, a better car or house, something more fashionable, some diet, some more fast food, the newest video game. The media fare we consume is supported by advertising. All the rest—what is referred to as "content"—is there to fill the spaces between one ad and the next.

We do not live naturally. We live unnaturally.

Because our minds are mediated by predator minds, ours become the prey, the victims. We live in an influence-or-be-influenced world.

In a traditional society, we are tyrannized by tradition—traditional ways of thinking, being, doing, having, and saying. In a modern society, we are tyrannized by fashion—fashionable ways of thinking, being, doing, having, and saying.

We may profess to be different. But we are all exposed to the same mass media messages and images. We are aggregated by what is current and popular. We have to differentiate within the parameters offered there.

We think the thoughts that others think. That's the material we have to work with. We become more like others because we consume the same media fare—especially mass advertising.

Television advertisements (and we do consume at the rate of four-plus hours a day) are usually in story form. We consume the stories and inadvertently their premises. For example, it's far better to be good looking than not. Victoria's Secret has no models who look like anyone you know. But the ones you know are trying. They try by buying—by buying both the implicit messages and the product.

Advertisers tell you the kind of life you should have. And then they tell you how you could have that kind of life.

Anyone who is addicted to the stories and images available en masse has only two choices:

1. To do life according to the massive almost irresistible normative forces that prey upon all of us indiscriminately, or
2. To do life by choice in spite of those forces.

Be forewarned: normative forces—small or large—usually win.

In ages past, there was no *law of large numbers*. All statistics is very modern. People used to have direct contact with all the members of their tribe or community. Now the people who most influence us are like the celebrities we idolize or the experts we believe. We don't know them personally, only by the publicity manufactured to support their celebrity.

Or, they are anonymous. When we are addressed by an advertising or canned political message, we don't know the people behind them. We can trust them—or not. But we cannot know them.

There certainly were norms in the smaller communities that preceded our urban and secular existences. Some were more restrictive than in our own permissive society. Hawthorne's *The Scarlet Letter* and the witchcraft travesties (as well as the "Crusades") are good examples. People often enforced their beliefs in violent ways.

LEE THAYER

Whether in a circle of friends or the larger society, people will always harbor their beliefs. They will pass judgment on others in keeping with their personal beliefs. The more widespread a belief, the more it takes on the mantle of a truth.

People have always fought for and defended their beliefs. You were not born with beliefs for which you would risk your life or your reputation. They had to come from your culture, even if they are contrary to others' professed beliefs.

Your beliefs may change if you change your cadre of endorsers. Most people don't change their cadre of endorsers. Their beliefs would be in jeopardy, as would their very identities.

Beliefs dominate our lives. If they lead us in the wrong direction, so be it.

What's behind the law of large numbers is that in large numbers people's beliefs are like a force of nature. Resist and you will likely cease to exist. (That's the way it worked for the American Indian.)

If such thoughts are not a part of your foundation for understanding the art of *doing life*, you will meet resistance that you cannot deal with.

We have to make a life in the context of *deficit-everything*. Deficit spending is one thing. But a philosophy of life which is mainly about deficit—about what's wrong with us and what needs fixing—attacks us where we live and not just how we live.

Our dominant mode of thinking about psychology—which derives mainly from Freud, is a deficit psychology. Something has to be wrong before we pay attention to it. As we will see later on, the so-called Morita psychology (Morita was a contemporary of Freud's) has the opposite orientation. The underlying logic is not about what we don't have or what's wrong with us psychologically, but about how to make the best of what we *do* have. These are radically different orientations. And they have radically different consequences for the way we do—or *could* do—life.

We are a *problem*-oriented culture. We float downstream in the maelstrom of our problems. We know other people mainly by their problems, not their aspirations. The news is about anomalies and negatives. If something goes wrong, it is reported. If something goes right, it is not.

We build our cultural trajectory out of our troubles and our problems. We seemingly don't know how to be responsible for our health or our problems. We pay to have them fixed—whether that is a doctor or a politician or some other expert. We look for our salvation from our celebrities (e.g., Oprah).

We seem to think that freedom is irresponsibility. We thrive on the negative. Listen in on most conversations. We are building a civilization of infinite troubles and negatives.

How to do life with such irrepressible forces at work? How to learn how to do things in a way which is contrary to the way things are done? As Jean-Paul Sartre put it (in *No Exit*, 1946):

> "*Hell is—other people!*"

Doing life well when social trajectories lie in the opposite direction is certainly not easy. It is not for the faint-hearted. You will be punished in some way for not being modal. It is not for the quick-fix consumers.

Doing life in ways that are beneficial for one's own best self-interests and simultaneously for the best interests of the collective (and is also benign) requires grown-ups. It requires *duty*—a sense of being responsible for the outcomes of doing life.

What Lincoln said back in 1862 seems even more pertinent today:

> "*In times like the present, men should utter nothing*
> *for which they would not willingly be responsible*
> *through time and in eternity.*"

Doing life well requires that you are responsible for the consequences.

The historian, sociologist, and equal rights advocate W.E.B. Du Bois had it right when he wrote:

> "*Responsibility is the first step in responsibility.*"

LEE THAYER

Our technologies make it necessary for us to change our lives far more than any choices we might make to do so.

Oral stories are typically more compelling than are written or packaged stories. That's because they occur in the presence of the story-teller. If you are a parent or any other kind of leader, for example, do your teaching in person, not by texting or textbook. The coolness of academic prose speaks to its irrelevance.

Representations of human life—molded or painted—millennia ago changed our conceptions of ourselves in powerful and redirecting ways.

The mirror was a watershed for human culture. It enabled people to see themselves as they imagined others might see them.

Photography had an even greater impact on how we do life. Even infants are taught how to be *poseurs*—that is, how to do life as if you were on camera. We could imagine others' expectations and judgments prior to photography. But with photography and it descendants, we can now place ourselves in the eyes of the other. We can play the role of director of our own performance, both in public and in private.

We can lie like photographs lie. We can do our lives as if in a movie.

Movies are manufactured. Increasingly, so are we.

But who teaches us how to do this? How should we be doing life in our own and our civilization's best interests? Technologies—even today's G-phones and all of the so-called social media—are wholly indifferent to these kinds of questions.

Technology will not save us from taking the wrong path. You have to save yourself from the anonymity and enormity of millions of people who could care less what happens to you—or to us.

To the extent that we are mindful of it, we cannot inhabit any real world. To be mindful of any world inside or outside of us, we have to translate it into a *langue* (the French term) we understand and think with. To make things communicable, we have to transform them into something we can understand and talk about.

The world we inhabit is largely the world created in and for the purposes of human communication. Our realities are *communication realities*—imagined realities, believed realities, normative realities. They are the realities we can share with others who are capable of being mindful of them.

Freud was right about this. When we talk to ourselves or each other, we create both our heavens and our hells. We create the worlds we inhabit mentally and emotionally in how we talk about things—in how we *explain* things.

What we talk about when we talk about ourselves and our worlds creates us and those worlds.

Doing life well requires each of us to do that well. We can't have a life we can't talk about. And we can't talk about a life we can't imagine.

Our first responsibility is there—both to ourselves and to others. It must be that if and only if we perform our roles in society (and vis-à-vis ourselves) superbly can we be free to do as we wish. Freedoms that are not born and nourished in responsibility are a ride to hell.

A parting thought* from the poet W.H. Auden (in *Under Which Lyre,* 1946):

> *"Thou shalt not sit*
> *With statisticians nor commit*
> *A social science."*

---

*   Or an excellent perch from which to fly into the rest of the book.

LEE THAYER

I

. . . Time and Attention

"As leisure time increases,
so also boredom increases."

The notion of "time" has always intrigued and provoked humankind. What is it? We have always known about day passing into night and then back again to day. People have always been fascinated by the passing of time.

We can keep time with our clocks and our calendars. There are instances when we are indifferent to time. There are other moments when time seems to be the most important thing in our lives.

We know it is relative to what we are doing. We know that it is tyrannical and unforgiving. If you miss your train, you have missed your train.

Some tried to make actions at work go like clockwork. That didn't work.

In the West, we think of time as a trajectory from the past to the future. The anthropologists who have lived with and studied the Trobriand Islands people have described their concept of time as a "puddle." You step into it, you step out of it. But it is always just like it was. For the American Indian and others, time was cyclical. Things always ended up where they began. You lived and you died. There were cycles in nature. The more you attuned yourself to the cycles of time—like circadian rhythms—the better your life.

Westerners see life and time as linear. We believe in progress. Even our histories are linear. So we think of our lives as linear—beginning somewhere, being present only fleetingly, and providing a future about which we can hope and dream.

The Australian Aborigine (for many thousands of years) sang the same songs their ancestors sang when they went on their "walk-abouts." Life was not about the future. It was about the past. It was not about what *could* be known. It was about what had forever been known.

As a concept, time is culturally specific. How you perceive time depends upon what culture you have been brought up in and what's going on.

For lovers, time "stops still"—that is, its passing is immaterial given what is going on between them. Warriors from our past tell us that a life or death engagement blocks out any thought of passing time completely.

So we also know that time is always relative to the activity we are engaged in. If we stare at a clock, time goes slowly (or so it seems). If we are fully absorbed in what we are doing, we lose all sense of time. People who are awaiting the boarding call for their flight glance at their watches frequently and nervously. Everything seems to be happening in slow motion. Clasping a loved one at the end of the flight is as timeless as it is transient.

Whatever else it may be, time is an irresolvable paradox.

Still, as a practical matter, we Westerners (increasingly, most people) will go on

- *Punctuating* our lives by *what* we put on our agendas, and *when*. Removed from the tides and the cycles of nature or of tradition, we punctuate our lives artificially—by the ubiquity of calendars and time pieces. Even your cell phone can "tell" you what time it really is, in case your enchantment in something in the present moment causes you to lose track of time.
  Primitive peoples would have considered this intolerable—this being tyrannized by clock and calendar time—in much the same way that we modern folk might consider their slavishness to their cycles of nature or tradition intolerable.
  But *punctuate* our lives we moderns must. Otherwise our lives might feel like a "puddle." The Trobriand Islanders were reported to have been much happier in general than we seem to be. Could this have anything to do with our fear of getting out of sync?

Time is our master. It seems we merely show up on time.

- We *regulate* our lives by clock-time and by the Gregorian calendar, as if not to do so would put an end to the forward movement of things. Our moments of feeling most alive are those in which we have fallen out of time.

  To be free apparently comes at the cost of letting something be in control other than ourselves. Otherwise we might feel out of control.

  The tallest building in our early urban collectives had—after its invention—a clock that all could observe. A whistle or a horn coordinated with the clock told us when to go to work and when to stop working. It used to be—and still is to a lesser extent—that work bringing the hay into the barn had to go on into the night if tomorrow it was going to rain. We have progressed. Today we can work 24/7 whether we are accomplishing anything vital or not.

  Having a clock enables us to measure value by time, making any other accomplishment of value seem secondary.

  We know the most valuable things are timeless. But we may have to check our wristwatches just to see if we are giving scheduled things their due.

  It's possible that what may be critical to the quality of our individual lives or our collective destiny has been occluded by the omnipresence of calendars and timepieces.

  Yes, our efforts have to be coordinated. But to what end? Technologies turn our means into our ends. This is nowhere more evident than what has become the master, and who the slave.

  In a chain-gang, every prisoner was manacled to the other prisoners at the ankle. We've made progress. We manacle ourselves to others by our wrists and our glances.

  We may have once wondered where we humans came from and where we are going. Now what we most need to know is what time it is.

Most lives these days are *punctuated* by other people, by other events. And most lives are *regulated* by clock time. Subjective time has to be deferred to leisure, which has its own problems.

It's intriguing to speculate on the fact that most of the 75 billion or so people who preceded us on this earth did so without the benefit of time-*telling* devices. What *were* they thinking? And on what *schedule*?

> *"This time, like all times, is a very good one,*
> *if we but know what to do with it."*
> —Ralph Waldo Emerson

Time provides us with two troubling problems.

The first is small, often trivial, quite commonplace, but vexing none the less. These are the problems that arise when we personally get out of sync with our intended schedules, or with others' schedules.

You forget an appointment. Your flight is cancelled. Now you have to rearrange everything. You are placed on hold: "Please hold for the next available agent." You're late for your dinner appointment, and there is no seating available. You contemplate some life insurance. But this is betting. You're betting that you will outlive the actuarial table. The insurance company is betting that you won't.

And so on and on. These problems arise every day, in every way. They are troublesome. Sometimes they are *vital* to life well lived.

The second problem is more serious, more consequential. It is the problem that arises when we ask ourselves at some juncture in our lifetimes if we are where we had hoped to be at this time in our lives.

There are many and varied *concepts* of time—invented by ambitious scholars and academicians attempting to achieve hegemony with their proprietary concepts. There are many *philosophies* of time—created by thinkers over the course of history who thought long and hard about what other philosophers said, and offered their own take on it.

Scientists would like to own the answer, as would poets. These are all *abstract* concepts of time. Then there is *objective* time—what you observe when you consult a reliable clock or watch. Like a *temporal* GPS system, this locates you not in space but in time. The more sophisticated technological gadgets can alert you to where you ought to be going in the next few minutes, and who is going to be waiting for you.

All these tricks may be practically useful, but they are still abstract.

There is also the subjective *experience* of time, which is not abstract but tangibly real to the individual. Serious painters and composers typically do not have a clock hanging on the wall. They do not work by clock-time.

When people are wholly engaged in what they are doing, time is irrelevant. When they are not, clock-time becomes significantly more important. And yet, an egg does not boil faster if you watch it.

A boxer is much more concerned about the opponent's next move than about what time it is. It requires an indifference to time to enjoy a great meal—or physical intimacy.

We adapt to clock time. But clock time and the subjective *experience* of time are not mutually obligatory. The clock doesn't care whether you observe it or not. It's a very one-sided relationship.

Timepieces have their invaluable and ubiquitous uses in Western civilization. But don't blame that on the clock. We belong to our technologies (particularly timepieces) far more than they belong to us. Try ignoring them for any prolonged period of time when other people are involved.

Doing life intentionally requires that subjective time must be the ruler. When clock-time dominates your life, the quality of your life is diminished. If we are to live in a world that is dominated by the rationality of clock-time, we may feel we have no choice if we are to participate in that world. But it may be useful to consider the fact that we have to adapt to it. It does not adapt to us.

The struggle between the subjective and the social—between the internal and the external—is as old as human existence. How you work it out may well determine whether or not it is you doing life—or life doing you.

There are two clocks that measure irrevocably the passage of people time. One is your biological clock. There is little you can do about that. The other is your mental clock—what you have on your mind. This is the source of your life at any age.

One thing seems inevitable:

> *If you are going to do life as you would have it,*
> *you must be the master of time, not its slave.*

Attention

It has long been understood that *we are a product of what we pay attention to.* We can only pay attention to what is somehow meaningful to us. What is meaningful to us is largely provided by the culture we belong to. We may improvise, but only within what seems acceptable to others who belong to that same culture.

We represent that culture in our thinking, our feelings, and our actions. That is the price of our membership in that culture.

What we pay attention to—and how we do so—are clearly more important than mere time. For good or ill, we are the product of what we attend to and how we explain it to ourselves and others. We are in the loop that originates in our culture and returns thus sullied by us to our culture.

Cultures change slowly as a result of how the people within them explain things. The intoxication of falling in love is one thing. The cumulative effects of being married for several years is quite another. Lovers wallow in their illusions, delusions. Older married couples are more likely to be critical of one another. Early-on, feelings are more important than facts. Later-on, facts—real or imagined—take precedence over feelings.

It is the cultures we belong to—whether of two people or of millions—that enable us to make things meaningful . . . or not. If they are violated unilaterally, they begin to disintegrate. Outside of some culture, the human world is inexplicable. Falling out of love has no explanation that is plausible to the other person.

Playwrights, poets, and writers have tried to bring this to our attention for many years. Beckett, for example, and Octavio Paz. In his famous novel, *War and Peace*, Leo Tolstoy wanted to tell us the truth about people (which he also thought to be impossible). About his character Platon Kataaev he wrote:

> *"Every word and every action of his was the expression*
> *of a force uncomprehended by him, which was his life."*

We have to understand in the abstract. But we have to do life concretely. We can better understand how things ought to be than how they actually come about. Somewhat earlier in the same novel, Tolstoy wrote:

> *". . . labels . . . serve to give a name to an event, and*
> *like labels, they have the least possible connection*
> *with the event itself."*

What we call a thing is never the thing itself, as Alfred Korzybski famously said. What gets us into trouble is mistaking the name or the label for the thing itself. In doing so, we miss the reality which, in the end, will have its way with us.

That is the practical matter in the way we talk about things or express ourselves. What we profess is never who we are. It is never who we will become. What we call things is a form of self-deception. If we want to communicate with one another, we have to call things by *some* name or label.

Saying "I love you" does not in any way guarantee love everlasting (whatever that might be). It is merely an invitation to the dance.

"And they lived happily ever after . . ." is a pleasing if commonplace way to end a story. But it is *never* the end of that story.

If you want to know what people might mean by what they say, you cannot rely on what they say. You have to observe what they *do*. Thus the best way to think about life is to observe how it is *done*, not how it is talked about. The only possible way of having the sort of life you desire is by *doing life* in that way. Talking about it or reading about how to do it may grease the conversational gears. But it has no connection to any actual life, as Tolstoy said.

You must pay attention not to what people say, but to what they do and how they do it. You must pay attention not to what you say, but to what you do. Actual lives are made of doing, not of talking.

The best way to explain yourself to yourself is by what you *do*. The best way to explain yourself to others is by what you *do*. The best way for others to explain themselves to you is by what they *do*, not what they say. What they say is an abstraction. The reality of their lives as they impact you does not lie in what they say, but only in what they do.

The columnist and wit Esar Evan gave us a nicely convoluted way of thinking about all this:

> *"When a woman marries, she gives up the attentions of several men for the inattention of one."*

The little twist is humorous. But there are two quite profound implications:

- One is that the protocols, institutions, and norms of doing life in any culture do not necessarily have the consequences we assume. Courting requires attentiveness. But the purpose of courting is something else. So if you follow where the path leads, you will necessarily lose the attentiveness that goes with flirting, courting, etc. You may have the romantic idea of becoming an airline pilot. But in actuality, it's a pretty boring job these days.

- The other is that attention wanes over time. What attracted your attention in the first place gives way to banality. Isn't the old saying something like "Familiarity breeds contempt"? When we get what we want, the attention we paid to getting it dissipates. Attention that is grounded in an illusion fades when the illusion fades. It is the pursuit of the prize that focuses our attention. Getting it diffuses both the attention and the heightened sense of life that accompanied the pursuit.

There is the person and then there is the *idea* of that person. Pay attention to the person, not your image of that person.

There is the event and then there is your concept—your label—for that event. Pay attention to the event, not your explanation of it.

It is when you mistake your mental model of the person or the event that you create problems—for yourself and for others. Doing life well does not require you to choose one over the other.

Doing life—as we will develop that vital process in this book—requires you to imagine what life at its fullest could be. Then it requires the capacity to change your immediate reality in an enabling direction. Once the reality around you supports what you *ought* to be, the life you ought to be doing is possible. To paraphrase Churchill, and to extend what St. Exupery wrote in his most provocative book, *The Wisdom of the Sands*, you first have to invent the contexts of your life. Then *they* will invent *you*. It's a logic that can only be played in that direction.

The best part of any journey is preparing for it, provisioning for it, and the attention given to maintaining your course.

Doing life well thus has to be a journey that has no ending.

If two lovers quarrel, you might guess either that they have already arrived at their destination, or that one or both had lost sight of the fact that life is not a destination, but a journey.

When attention flags, so does the meaning of life. People seek respite from the meaninglessness of their own lives by escaping into some way of killing time—some involvement or activity to which they have become addicted that only temporarily demands their attention.

> *The difference between doing life successfully or unsuccessfully depends upon how passionately one attends to what needs attending to in order to do life rather than to be done-to by life.*

> *To paraphrase an old adage: "Show me what a person pays attention to and I can tell you what kind of life that person has."*

It isn't time that matters so much. It is what you do with it. And that amounts to the relevance of what you give your attention to, and how capable you are of doing so.

Careless or indifferent attention to the people or the events that may be crucial to your present or your future leads to a careless and indifferent life.

[This piece and the pieces that follow are not like chapters that build upon the previous piece. Each is a separate short essay about themes that are relevant to doing life as you would have it done.

Certain of these themes appear in different contexts in more than one of the pieces of the book. They are not there to be repetitive. They are there because they are fundamental to the depth of your understanding—your Return on Attention, for example. So please pay heed! You have not encountered them before in the particular context in which they may appear later.]

II

. . . Choices and Decisions

"In literature as in love, we are astonished
at the choices made by other people."

—Andre Maurois

The Hungarian-born, U.S.-educated 20th-century psychiatrist Thomas Szasz was well-known for his unorthodox views about mental health. Like R. D. Laing, for example, he once suggested that it could be the conventional, conforming people who were insane, not those who had been locked up for disagreeing or misbehaving with respect to the larger culture.

Szasz asked us to consider three very important points for our purposes in this book:

- One is that there is no guarantee that the beliefs of the majority are going to take us where we ought to be going, let alone protect us from our own self-inflicted demise. The fact that most of the major civilizations of the past no longer exist should lead us to question our belief that we are evolving in the best of all possible directions.

- Second, as the playwright/philosopher George Bernard Shaw put it—we owe all progress to those who are unreasonable. This is as true in science as in the arts and medicine and social life in general. One may have to violate conventional beliefs in order to make a more valuable contribution.

- Third, and perhaps most important, we may not be able to preclude the physical calamities that befall some people. But our mental state is something that we people make. In the choices and decisions we make every day, we establish a trajectory for our lives—individually and collectively—that cumulatively empowers itself.

Here's the way Szasz (in one of his more introspective moments) described a very modern proclivity in *The Second Sin*:

> *"People often say that this or that person has not yet found himself. But the self is not something one finds. It is something that one creates."*

And, as he and others well understood, that creation is a matter of the small choices and decisions you make every day. They are cumulative. A choice changes you. You make your next choice from that condition, not from any previous one.

All growth—particularly the growth of the mind—is irreversible. The consequences of our minute choices may be small. But they culminate in who we are at any moment.

Within the limits of what's available, we choose what we eat, we choose where we go, we choose how to respond in even the most banal conversation, we choose our friends and our life partners. There is even a sense in which we choose how to react to what happens to us—as Eleanor Roosevelt reminded us.

In making our choices—out of the material available to us from our own minds, which are in turn derived from culture and the subcultures to which we choose to belong, and from our interpretations of our past experiences—we are indirectly but inevitable choosing the form and destiny of our lives down the road.

There are no inconsequential choices. All of our choices, from the smallest to the largest, have consequences—for us, and often for others or the larger society. On a given day, we choose what to wear from what we have available. That choice will have consequences. You may not have considered what those consequences might be.

You do not control the consequences. You control only the choices you make.

To make any real choice, you have to have whatever it takes on your part and on the part of others (that is, the rest of the world) to produce the consequences you desire. Otherwise, you are merely deluding yourself.

Merely to want this or that for yourself is not a *choice*. It's empty rhetoric. That's probably why most people are disappointed in their choices. The motivational speakers people pay attention to say dream big—want it badly enough and you will succeed. It doesn't work that way in the real world.

You may harbor your secret hopes and dreams. But you have to do life in the real world.

You may even ask or expect someone else to make you happy. But everyone else in the world has their own agenda. Millions of things have happened in the past that produced the present context. Billions of people are busy doing their own thing at this moment (not yours).

You can read a book about being successful, or about having a better life. Such books can produce a temporary recipe and an elevated feeling of self-confidence. But your intentions are at best no more than a means to an end.

If you can't imagine in considerable detail the world in which you intend to do your life, you won't be able to do it there. If you are not equipped to do the heavy lifting of fixing your outside world to make it at least *possible* to do the life you envision in it, it's almost wholly unlikely to happen.

This may not be inspiring. But the reality is that the rest of the world is not continuously inspired to enable *you* to do the life you envision in it. Most other people are indifferent to your dreams and wishes. Another may be promising to fulfill your life when you are standing at the altar. But after a while, even the best marriages seem to grow stale, unable to fulfill two individual egos.

Wanting a better life is laudable. But you have to be *competent* to bring it off in the context of a world full of people doing things that are independent of, and maybe even opposed to, your interests. The experts don't tell you that. They are predators and you are their prey. Why would they let you in on *their* secrets? It would only ruin the game for them.

The consequences of billions of people doing their own lives are in your life like a force of nature. No one knows what those consequences are going to be. It's far too complex.

But this is the world in which you have to do your life. To emphasize, *you will either do life or life will do you.*

Let us go back to the epigraph from Maurois at the head of this chapter:

> *"In literature as in love, we are astonished at the choices made by other people."*

Or, we could add, in everyday life as well. Our own choices usually make perfectly good sense to us. But the choices of others often puzzle us. Why *did* they choose to do what they did?

What's implicit here can be very useful in thinking about doing one's own life.

- It is easy for you to *justify* your own choices. You can add all kinds of good reasons—before, during, or after the fact.
- We are not as open to accepting others' justifications (or rationalizations) as we are our own.
- But here's the crux of the matter:

  Most of the choices people make most of the time are conjured up from inner sources others are not privy to. They are often convoluted. They are rarely as rational as we might like to believe. They are usually based on *feelings*—not facts. They are more likely to be arrived at impulsively and automatically, not deliberately. So, as observers, we are stuck trying to comprehend an action rationally, when it was not a rational act in the first place.
  Love, as above, is a good example. Why did these two people get together? Feelings were involved, and feelings are not rational. So we can't know why. Only they know why. And they don't know why any more than you do.

They will justify their actions if those around them will buy those justifications.
Because of how they are arrived at, choices are not objectively analyzable. They have to be evaluated solely on the basis of their consequences.

But this leads us to something even more valuable to our thinking about doing life. It is that it may not be the choice itself that matters so much. It is far more likely to be how the choice was implemented.

Competent people have a way of transforming poor choices into good consequences. Incompetent people by much the same logic have a way of turning even good choices into undesirable consequences. So the most important aspect of any choice is how capably it was implemented.

And that in turn reveals two more implications of potential value:

- One is that people who are less than competent to carry out a choice will be unwilling even to consider it. Thus those who most need to make life-changing choices are typically the least capable of doing so. They may be the ones who are most dissatisfied with their lives. They may entertain the loftiest goals in life. But they cannot make a plan that they could execute. *You simply can't change people who can't change themselves.* And this would include you.
  Psychiatrists and psychotherapists—not to mention teachers and parents and spouses and friends—have known this forever. Everyone involved may be well-intentioned. But an intention is not the same thing as an accomplishment.
  As a species, humans may be infinitely malleable by their social environments. But individually the objectives sought by some individual choice must offer an overwhelmingly greater return on investment than that individual's own status quo—their familiar comfort zones. And this is going to happen only if *they* have the kind of competence and commitment to bring it about.
  Trying to inspire or motivate them never increases competence, and may heighten the desire to be committed, but it does not increase their commitment in any permanent way. "*Talk does not cook rice,*" as the Chinese proverb has it.

- Of equal value to your approach to doing life is this: Thinking (talking privately to oneself) does not exist in any real world. It exists only in the mind of the mind of the person doing the thinking. You can't know in any direct way what other people are thinking. All you have to go on is what they say and what they do about what they say. In short, how they behave. And, most importantly, that's all they have to go on when observing you. Other people have no access to your thinking. Your choices are made in your mind, not theirs. Thus you must take great care that your performance is understood as you would have it understood. Do not permit them to interpret you from the perspective of *their minds. Explain yourself before, during, and after if you want your choices to be implemented.* If you don't, let them speculate. But make it necessary that they speculate in the direction that most benefits your purposes in being the one who does your own life. You can't change people directly. But *if* you make it *necessary* for them to interpret you and your actions on your terms, you will have maximized your influence over them.

  Now think through doing this for yourself. Interpret your choices and your actions in such a way that those interpretations will get you where you want to go. This takes practice. But *that's what life is—practicing for doing life.*

  If you can do that, you will optimize the possibilities of doing life the way you would have it done.

Keep in mind that **choice** is greatly overrated. You do not choose a spouse based on a representative sample. You choose the one who will have you. And he or she is drawn from a very, very small sample.

There is no guarantee that the one you choose will choose you for any of the right reasons. Whatever they may promise, most people are very self-centered. They are in the game for their own reasons, which are never truly known by the other person.

Choice, as illusory as it is, is almost never independent of the complicity of other people. And they have their own agendas. You might imagine that it was your choice. But the other person may have made the choice—and for his or her own reasons. You and the other chooser just happened to come together at the right time. Even so, it is always best to assess choices in terms of their consequences.

And you cannot know in advance what those consequences will be. As in life as in love, you have to make the leap. Promises are not guarantees. They are merely a move in a game that furthers the game.

> No choice is really made until there are consequences.
> And the meaning and value of the choice is determined
> by the consequences.

In one of his many letters, the Prague-born poet Rainer Maria Rilke wrote as follows:

> "A good marriage is that in which each appoints the
> other guardian of his solitude"

In other words, they do not want to know the other literally. It is the other's solitude that holds the possibilities of wonder, of love, of caring. We moderns are far too psychological in our thinking and our decisions. We like to pretend that we can read the other's mind. That, as so many have found to their dismay, is a killer of what we call love.

The primary reason why choice is so overrated is alluded to in this quip from the humorist Evan Esar:

> "A man picks a wife about the same way an apple
> picks a farmer."

You may have to think about this one. It's a challenging metaphor. But then so is life a challenging and prolific web of metaphors, which holds us in its embroidery.

Those who cannot do metaphors usually find it frustratingly beyond their powers to try to do life as it could be done.

Apples don't pick a particular farmer—or even a particular apple tree. It just happens. Apple trees produce apples because that's what they do. The farmer may be a superior nurturer of apple trees, But not even the farmer can choose the apples that grow on his or her tree.

Life is like that. We do what we are capable of doing. We can't choose to do life. It will be done the way we (if we are the trees) are built. To produce apples, we would have to be an apple tree. To do life means that the life we do will be an inevitable consequence of who we *are*.

You have to *be* something in order to *do* something. And the something that you will do will be an inevitable function of who you *are*. The life you can do will always be a function of the person you are. <u>Make yourself into the person you would need to be in order to *do* the life you envision</u>.

Then you will have chosen that outcome.

So an interpretation of the metaphor above might be—

> *A person chooses a life in the same way an apple*
> *chooses an apple tree.*

If you cannot make *inevitable* the life you would like to have, you cannot "choose" it.

We give choice too much credit. And we give all that's required for the choice to be realized too little.

The factors that play upon the choice only begin with your commitment. If you cannot use those other factors for your purposes, your choice will likely remain stillborn. The world is an ongoing story made up of millions of sub-stories. How does your choice fit into those?

Everything evolves out of what exists. If there are formidable forces at work (such as the larger culture or major sociopolitical forces elsewhere), your choice may not have much of a chance to be realized.

Your choice has to be compelling to the person or the people who have to be complicit in making it happen. Others need to play a role in bringing it off. They have to be competent in their role and willing to help you fulfill your cause. The spread of any religion would be a good example.

So you have to be committed, and you have to get others in supporting roles committed to the story the way you want it to turn out. Otherwise, you will not be the author but a bit player in a story you didn't compose.

A choice without the means to carry it out is nothing but wishful thinking. It has no inevitability about it. You cannot *will* your choice into existence. You have to manipulate the means that will make it inevitable.

Given the way things are composed and how they come together, there is an inevitability about everything that happens. That is what you need in order to realize your choices. You need inevitability on your side. Otherwise, all you can hope for is luck.

To probe as deeply as possible into the heart of the matter—indispensable to anyone who would do life as opposed to being done-to—we might call upon one of the world's most extraordinary writers." Doris Lessing is not a comfortable writer. In fact, she is extraordinarily provocative. She puts a controversial point of view right in front of us and asks us to think about—to think deeply about it.

Here are three examples (from *Prisons We Choose to Live Inside*):

> *"It is possible to sit through hours, days, of discussion*
> *about war, and never hear it mentioned that one of*
> *the causes of war is that people enjoy it, or enjoy*
> *the idea of it."*

IF this is so,

- Why *do* people choose to enjoy it—or the idea of it?
- Why is it that we choose to enjoy war, but seem not to be able to tolerate peace?
- In the myth of the Garden of Eden, the first two humans got thrown out of Paradise. Why is it we can't choose Paradise over its many contraries?

- Why can't people talk about the fact that people seem to enjoy war? Even Shakespeare seemed to know that the best lovers were also the best antagonists.
- Do we have to create in reality the horrors of war in order to fantasize and compose popular songs about "when it's over, over there"? That's a perverted set of choices, isn't it?
- But who's to say that human minds are not a perversion of nature?

There are also behind movements such as feminism the unquestioned certitude—

"... that women are more peaceable than men. History does
not exactly bear this out."

- Why do we choose beliefs over facts?
- Why are mass movements based upon falsehoods (such as Socialism)?
- Why do smart people do dumb things?
- Why is it that our own human best self-interests get submerged by whatever is fashionable in our thinking and our feelings?

Or consider this as a collective choice:

"... for two thousand years Europe was under a tyrant—the
Christian church—which allowed no other way of thinking,
cut off all influences from outside, did not hesitate to kill,
extirpate, persecute, burn and torture in the name of God."

- Quite apart from the validity of Christianity, why did the people who tortured or burned other human beings *choose* to do this?
- The Nuremburg trials were all about this: why did the people who turned on the gas in the gas chambers *choose* to do so? Were they merely obeying a higher authority, or did they actually enjoy the power over others it afforded?
- Why did the saints who ran the church demand this tyranny?
- Does the truth justify the persecution of others? Was the mass murder of Aborigines in Australia (or America) justified by the fact that the people with the guns were superior human beings?

- What would it *mean* to be a superior human being?
- Don't most conflicts and violence erupt between right and wrong even in marriages and bars and hockey matches? Why do people *choose* to drift into violence?
- Why is it that even people who know the right thing to do often don't do the right thing?

Is an ideological choice actually a choice? Or does conformity (with one's crowd) trump choice?

We are trapped in the consequences of the choices made by people we never knew because they lived before us, or because they function anonymously. Collective movements have their own inertial forces. Whatever enables them to gain traction, they seem to live on past their own aims.

Blacks have done well in America since the slavery involved in owning other people was outlawed. They have done better than poor whites. So why do they choose to posture still as victims? How much more liberation do women need? Where do these public sentiments come from? And why do people choose into them?

We are pushed and pulled by the collective choices made years ago, or presently. Most people are content to have it this way. We are content with the *tyranny of fashion*—in thinking and believing, in being and having, and in doing.

Is it possible to *do life* in or out of *some* tyranny? People seemingly cannot handle too much freedom to choose from a surfeit of possibilities (the "paradox" of choice). Where anything is possible anything will happen. Who is supposed to be in charge in a secular, democratic society? Is a slavish dedication to whatever is popular less a form of slavery than any other?

> *If a choice is a choice only in its consequences, how can one know the right choice without being responsible for the consequences?*
> *Is **irresponsibility** a right guaranteed by the Constitution?*
> *How free should one be to choose if the choice impacts other people negatively?*
> *If a pupil disrupts a class, is that a right?*

If someone's lifestyle puts his or her life in jeopardy, which
must be paid for by other people, is that a free choice?
Does my right to choose end where it impinges upon yours?

These are age-old questions. There are no easy answers. But they are very much worth thinking hard about if one intends to do life in the context of others doing their lives—collectively and/or individually.

Decisions

Everything that has been said about choices applies to decisions. These days decisions are likely to involve more than one person. They are likely to be more deliberative. And they are likely to be more subject to the claims of rationality or objectivity.

In an ongoing conversation, what a person chooses to say next is not really a choice. It will be a matter of habit, of handy clichés or fashionable expressions, or of the individual's sense of propriety. *People say what is said,* as the philosopher Ortega y Gasset suggested.

A decision, like a choice, is not "made" until there are consequences. Then the meaning or the right/wrongness of the decision can be judged. The dilemma here is that *we can only understand things that are past, but we have to live life going forward.* (Another pragmatic philosopher at work, this time Martin Heidegger.) We all know this, but most people seem not to acquiesce to the irrefutable logic. We can't understand what our actions will produce in the future because the future hasn't happened yet. Marriage partners have struggled with this dilemma for millennia.

As has often been observed throughout history,

> *Truth is to the understanding what music is to the ear,*
> *or beauty is to the eye.*

No belief or theory or proclivity—or decision—is right or wrong apart from its consequences.

Doing life does not have to do with choice or decision. It has to do with the consequences of what is done or not done. Life and its "doing" are inseparable. The one defines the other.

What is true is what gets us where we're going. But what is false will get us somewhere else just as fast.

Right or wrong are both false gods. This has never stopped us from perceiving the world this way. Nor has it stopped us from giving our lives for some cause.

Yet belief is indispensable. As Felipe Fernandez-Armesto reminded us in his book Truth,

> ",,,when people stop believing in something, they do not believe in nothing; they believe in anything."

The door to anything is opened with the keys of choice.

The Irish novelist, poet, and dramatist Oliver Goldsmith should perhaps be given the last word:

> *"When I have made up my mind I always listen to reason because it can then do me no harm."*

One might wonder why he would *choose* to say it so reasonably, or how any reader might *choose* to interpret it. Do people *ever* listen to reason?

Some people choose to be competent. At least we assume that was their choice. Some people choose to be incompetent. If competence is a choice, so is incompetence. If incompetence is not a choice, then neither is competence a choice. They are either both choices, or neither is.

The back-story question is: On what basis do people choose one way of life rather than another? Why would you?

III

. . . Roles and Rules

"All the world's a stage,
And all the men and women merely players:
They have their exits and entrances:
And one . . . in his time plays many parts."

—Shakespeare, *As You Like It*

On the façade of Shakespeare's Globe Theatre was written, *Totus Mundus Agit Histrionem*— "all the world is a theatre." The point was that everyone, everywhere, is playing a *role* in some ongoing story. That is the source of the structure, the belief systems, and the evolution of all relationships, all societies.

Sammy Davis, Jr. was not referring to the movie set "lights, camera, action" when he remarked:

"As soon as I go out the front door of my house in the
morning, I'm on, Daddy, I'm on."

He may have been one of the first to use the expression, "to be on." What he meant, apparently, was that when he went out into the public, he looked at himself as a character in a play because this was the way others were going to look at him. When other people are present, he is on-stage. When they are not, he continues to review and prepare to conduct himself the way he imagines his fans imagine *him* as a character in their story of him.

When we take on the image that others have of us, we are playing a role in a story. We may influence that image others have of us by *how* we play the role given us to play. When we are in sync with others, we are now involved in theatre. When we are not, the social fabric begins to unravel.

This of course is what Erving Goffman was getting at in his book, *The Presentation of Self in Everyday Life.* We "communicate" our role by how we dress, coif, and comport ourselves in the presence of others. In playing a role recognized and validated by others, we initiate a story, we move the story along, or we conclude the story in which all present are collaborating.

The following quotation from Stanford Lyman and Marvin Scott's book, *The Drama of Social Reality,* provides a succinct launching platform and underpinning for this chapter:

> *"Social reality . . . is realized theatrically. Otherwise put,*
> *reality is a drama, life is theatre, and the social world*
> *is inherently dramatic."*

We can and will improve on this. But it is a good way to launch this exploration of *roles* and *rules.* All human and social behavior is a performing art. We have to learn what the stories are that we will be called upon in which to assume a role. And we have to learn how to play those roles. None of this is in our genes.

As early as we can, we teach our babies how to *pose* for the camera. We augment our teaching with hours of examples from television (especially the commercials) about how to *pose* for the camera—which is a stand-in for other people. Not many of us will really be models. But we will pose as if we were.

We are taught how to see ourselves as others see us. This is preparation for playing the roles we will take on during our lifetimes.

Roles

Roles are always *reciprocal*—even if only in our imagination.

We are who we are because others are who they are. And we are who we are because others around us are collaborating with us in a story that involves all of us.

You can't be a friend unless you have a friend—and this requires being that other person's friend. No one is born knowing how to do this. You have to learn every role you inhabit. A lover requires a lover. A celebrity requires fans. We play our roles in the context of others playing *their* roles. We know in general the story we are in. How we play our role, and how others play their role, is what creates and furthers the story or scenario we assume ourselves to be in.

The network of people we want to belong to used to be referred to as our "reference group"—the group we refer our performances to in order to know whether we're playing our role right or not. They may be real. They may be imaginary. We refer our performance to them for judgment.

We judge ourselves of course, by internalizing the expected judgments of those to whom we refer our thoughts, feeling, and behavior. That's what a conscience is for. Our reference groups function as our *collective conscience*. Their judgment—real or imagined—usually trumps our own. When it does we are in trouble.

We can't belong unless we further the interests and values of the groups, cultures, and subcultures (the "reference groups") that we want to belong to. We enact the standard stories of the groups we belong to. If we have high status, we can add variations on those standard stories that will gain acceptance. If we have low status in those groups, variations are more likely to be considered violations.

We know generally what things mean because that's what they mean to the groups we belong to. Those meanings are implicit. They come to us by a sort of osmosis from the groups we belong to.

As the British anthropologist Mary Douglas wrote about the primitive peoples she studied in her 1975 book, *Implicit Meanings*:

> "It was evident that a very satisfactory fit, between the structure of thought and the structure of nature **as they thought it** (emphasis mine), was given in the way that their thought was rooted in community life."

Put another way, those people thought alike because they talked to each other. In talking to each other, they came to think alike. They created their social realities. It is those *social realities* that channel and guide human thought.

It is what things *mean* to you or me that guides our thinking, feelings, and actions.

The French scholar Emile Durkheim is generally credited with being one of the founders of the field of sociology. He is widely-known for his concept of "collective representations"—how groups of people come to share the same or similar meanings for things.

As Douglas and others have suggested, he was telling us that *our colonization of each other's minds is the price we have to pay for thought.* In other words, if you have a mind, it is because it has been and continues to be colonized by other minds—whether in a casual conversation, in reading or television consumption, or in terms of our collective mind. A "collective" mind is imbedded in our culture, our subcultures, and our circle of communicating friends and acquaintances. For the most part, it is our minds that constitute our reality.

We know *implicitly* what things mean because we create and maintain their meanings in talking about them to one another in the groups to which we belong. What things mean to us is always implicit. There are premises that undergird every statement. If you are a member-in-good-standing of some human group, you will internalize those premises. It is the premises that inform the meanings we impose on what is said and what is done.

What shall we say of conscience? Our consciences consist of whatever we internalize of the beliefs, orientations, perspectives, worldviews, and explanations that constantly swirl around us. It is our guide to thinking and feeling and doing what's expected when playing a role.

Native American Indians, in all of their 25,000-35,000 years on the North American continent, had perhaps fewer than a dozen different roles for people to learn and perform. We have several hundred in the occupational index alone. Socially, we have increasingly more.

Ours is an open society—open to whatever changes people make on purpose or by accident that becomes validated by others. Theirs was a closed society—channeled by traditions and rituals from the past. They were not open to changes that violated their ancient beliefs and traditions.

They believed in their past. We believe in our future—whatever we happen to make of it.

The fewer the roles available, the easier they are to learn. It also makes evaluating performance in those roles more stringent. When there are few roles, everyone else is an auditor. When there are many, then people become anonymous judges of our performance of our roles.

This of course is where social order comes from. Societies are ordered by the stories people assume they're in, and the roles they perform within those stories. The more repetitive those stories and the more ritualistic they are, the more social order there is. In small communities, it is easy to deduce others' working consciences by how they perform. They can be personally observed. The more people in our communities who consume certain television programs and commercials (for example), the more anonymous those people become and the less our personal sanctions and approval or disapproval matter one way or the other.

Small, closed societies are moralistic. Large, open societies are legalistic. This doesn't mean that one is better than the other. The Mafia had very rigid rules about right and wrong. There were severe punishments for waywardness.

Our heroes in America are often those who flaunt the rules. Speed limits are not observed because they don't have to be. A moralistic society is one based on have-to (a conscience thing). A legalistic society is more likely to be one in which you are wrong only if you get caught.

An affair in a moralistic society is more likely to be stopped before it can get started. It is more often stopped in a legalistic society only if you get caught.

Doing life in a moralistic society is very different from doing life in an infinitely-expanding and legalistic society.

The sociologist Talcott Parsons was one of the first of a long list of contemporary theorists who believed that **roles** rather than personalities should be the unit of analysis. We are extending and grounding that perspective in this book. And Erving Goffman set forth in several books (e.g., *The Presentation of Self in Everyday Life*) his conviction that the self is a performance. So we are in very good company here.

You are who you are because you *perform* your self in various ways. You *are* some conglomeration of all of the roles you have played in all of the stories or scenarios you assume you and others are involved in.

All of which brings us usefully to these conclusions:

- First, and as a reminder, we live simultaneously in three worlds (or environments):

    1. Our own bodies, which at any moment can betray us.
    2. The world of our own minds, which contain the virtual realities that we actually navigate by.
    3. The physical and social worlds outside of us, which are forever impacting us in ways we consider "random." What we know is that much of our suffering as well as our joys originate with other people and in that often unpredictable world outside of us.

- Second, any life you can have has to be had in the context of the roles and the stories that already exist as social conventions in your culture and subcultures; OR

- Third, if you even consider doing life outside of the constraints and opportunities that exist in your present environment(s), that would require the courage, the wherewithal, and the blind passion on your part to do so.

The fantasies most people have about who they would like to be—how they would prefer doing life—are stillborn. They begin and end in their imagination and in a few casual conversations.

You have to *perform* the role(s) you would have in life. Those performances have to be endorsed by those who would have to be supporting cast in the story you want to tell in doing your life your way (far easier sung than done).

You have to be capable of seducing yourself irrevocably into the plot required. And you have to be capable of seducing others into performing their roles in your story. A few people in history have done this—Gandhi comes to mind, but there was also Theodore Roosevelt and the mythical (or real) King Arthur and his "Camelot."

In other words, you would have to be capable of *leading* yourself and your needed accomplices out of the mindsets they presently depend upon into a new and different bunch of mindsets and worldviews, with the outcomes largely uncertain. That's what leaders do. That's how *they* do life. That's how you would have to do life, if you wanted one that was not merely given.

If you want to do life "your way," there are no other options. You will either have a minor role in existing stories (social conventions) or the lead role in yours. It will not be handed to you.

Doing life your way requires the same indomitable spirit evidenced by those artists who end up changing the way art is done and looked at—an outcome that was never guaranteed. The only guarantees come from doing life the way others want you to do it. And even then, the outcomes are uncertain.

Rules

The social rules that regulate any relationship or society are embedded in how people conceive of and play their roles in the stories they imagine they are in.

Because people must be relatively interchangeable with respect to the games they play—whether board games, social games, children's games, sports—there must be rules. To know how to play the game—even games of love and politics—you have to know the rules. It is the game that matters, not the players.

If there were rules for living, but no games, life would be fairly meaningless. The fact that we can lose at love or in business makes the game worth playing. It is the fact that we don't know who is going to win that makes games so seductive. It is the fact that people get penalized (sometimes extremely so) for breaking the rules that keeps the game itself alive.

Social games of all sorts are like this. Doing life is like playing an extended game. If we play within the rules, we can have a life, of sorts. If we don't play by the rules, we will end up outside of them.

There are generically two kinds of "rules":

- There are *prescriptive* rules—you must do this or that.
- There are *proscriptive* rules—you must *not* do this or that.

One of the best examples of social and sexual gaming you might ever be privy to is the film, *Liaisons Dangereuses* (Dangerous Liaisons) based on an 18th-century tale by Choderlos de Laclos. In it the two main characters scheme to use social conventions to exploit the people who live by them. It is a private game of seduction by two competitive people (a man and a woman) to determine which one can outwit the social conventions of the day. It is a game played about a game.

People who are virtuoso game-players (like world-class poker players) play by the rules, but they make moves that surprise their competitors. Jazz musicians do this regularly.

Advantage and innovation come from bending the rules. The best players take advantage of those who are less competent at using the rules to their advantage.

The rules of the game—including the most contemporary and emerging social games—level the playing field. But they do not level the players. Tournament tennis players play on the same court with the same rules. But one still wins, and one loses. An experienced courtesan can beat the novice would-be seducer at his own game.

In a commercial society such as our own the rules are *not* reciprocal. The person who would sell you something may be playing by a set of rules. But you are not playing by the same rules, and may not even know what the predator's rules are. The aim in a commercial transaction is for the seller to take money out of your pocket and put it in theirs.

Both can lie, of course. And both can haggle. But in a commercial transaction, the seller is the predator and the buyer is the prey. The predator always knows something the prey does not. This is the way it works in the wild. The predator has a strategy. If the prey cannot detect and counter that strategy with a protective or escape strategy of their own, the predator wins.

It is an unruly world. The players are free to use whatever deceptive tactics they can think up. A good car salesperson will make you think you got a "deal" no matter how much you overpaid. You will report to your friends what a good deal you manipulated in spite of how much you overpaid.

This commercial orientation has crept into the social games people play. When people appear in public, they are likely to use whatever deceptive tactics work—whether it is a look, a way of dressing, or a way of walking or talking. Increasingly, under the influence of the commercial media, we try out different personas.

I will pretend to be what you want if you will pretend to be what I want is not a solid basis for a good marriage, as the divorce statistics reveal. Money and power attract beauty. And beauty attracts money and power. If you don't have at least two of the three, you are stuck with being a spectator in the bleachers of the way the media present doing life.

We have made ourselves into commodities, to be bought and sold for whatever we have of value to the social marketplace.

At its most cynical, but probably the most practical, what this means is that the person with the most cunning wins. He who is merely competent doesn't. The notion of rules in social life is probably an antiquated one.

There is the story of two well-known and respected authors who bought 100,000 of their own book in order to get it listed on the best-seller list. That brought them a tidy profit and they still had 100,000 books to sell.

That's cunning. Machiavelli lived and wrote during that period of time when we were changing from an agrarian to a commercial society. He warned his prince that "all is fair in love and war," and that the prince needed to be more cunning—and more effective at it—than his adversaries.

His advice may be more pertinent today than it was in his time, simply because there still existed in his time the quaint notion that there is honor among thieves. Most of that has evaporated.

The satirical columnist Evan Esar's take on this was:

> *"It's a poor rule that won't work both ways, but a poorer one that won't work our way."*

Courtship used to have reciprocal rules, as Jane Austen played with seriously in her books. Now the rules are, as they are in commercial advertising: whatever works. We are no longer guided by tradition, but by who gets the better of whom.

We live in a world of having vs. being-had. If you intend to do life in this world, you have to be more cunning than those who would tell you how to do it.

Even your neighbors these days profess to know more about how you should live than you do. And the commercial media profess to know more than *they* do about how to live your life.

Doing life as you would have it done has always been *in spite of,* not because of these influences. Helped along by pop psychology, increasing numbers of people seem to prefer doing life as *victims.* They seek out causes for why they can't or won't. And we're buying it. We are creating a culture that prioritizes their needs over the needs of our civilization. These folk, creeping up on half the population, are not doing life. They are voting for those who will satisfy *their* needs.

We buy and sell our politicians by how we personally like their performances in the media. We don't learn how to think in school. We learn how to consume and how to posture ourselves. We don't know what the long-term issues in our world are, only those immediate and transient issues dramatized by the media.

We don't realize that the freedoms we purchase in one part of our lives has to be paid for by our imprisonment in another. David Riesman, the author famous for his characterization of people as either mainly inner-directed or other-directed in his 1950 book, *The Lonely Crowd*, wrote that people . . .

> *". . . lose their social freedom and their individual autonomy in seeking to become like each other."*

The commercial media and increasingly the rest of our pop culture do something like homogenizing us. We comply by seeking to look like and comport ourselves like our current celebrities and our neighbors. We don't fully realize that we are offering ourselves up as victims of the latest fads and fashions—if only they are about our toys for keeping in touch with one another. We want what is new. And we want it NOW.

This is a part of the real world in which you have to do life. You can't change it. But you need to be aware of that reality.

Maybe we don't seek to become like each other. We huddle together in our social media to differentiate ourselves. But as our minds shrink to fit the media and the way our computers and the media are programmed, we simply become more like each other.

Those who are addicted to the news and fashions of the day via the media are as readily manipulated as those who are addicted to drugs. The dealer has the power over you gained from having what you are addicted to.

> *Doing life in any but the conventional ways was always difficult. As life becomes less rule-bound and more adversarial, doing life as you would have it has become even more difficult.*

As the 17th-century poet John Donne scribed it:

> *". . . as to the bed's feet, life is shrunk."*

Life shrinks or enlarges according to the constraints or possibilities with which it has been endowed.

That is the context in which you have to make the choices you will need to make with respect to doing life as you would have it done.

IV

. . . Change and Stasis

"Nothing ever stays the same."

People are forever in the process of becoming who they are.

What this means is that you have a life, an identity, a self with all of its inherent limitations and possibilities. You *evolve*, usually in an adventitious way. You can only evolve out of what you are at any given moment. Who you *are* determines who you will become—unless you make disruptive choices.

Neither hope not desire can change the logic of this process. Only choices implemented under adversity can. What you cannot change about yourself is therefore a person you cannot become.

In the meantime the world around you is constantly changing. It, too, will follow the logic of becoming whatever is necessary out of whatever it is at the moment. Things are always in the process of becoming what they are.

It is crucial to remember this. You can only evolve out of what you are. You can never start over again. There is no way to wipe the slate clean. What you *have* become will always be the major determinate in what you will become.

Think of it this way: you have to evolve out of the circumstances—the raw material, actually—of what you already are. There are no exceptions. There are no other options. You have to do life out of what you happen to have to do so with. If you would be someone else, you have to change who you are—unless of course miraculously who you are will inevitably produce who you really want to be.

Most people seem not to realize that who they are today determines who or what they might become tomorrow. Tinkering with these inevitabilities means playing god with yourself. You have to become the Creator. No one else can do it for you. And what you envision is not going to happen naturally. Because "naturally" means that you have to evolve out of who you are.

In much the same way, most people seem to accept who they are. They just don't realize that this is also accepting the inevitability of who they will become out of who they are. You can't have it both ways. If you choose yourself as you are, you have chosen the trajectory of your life, however it evolves.

*You **cannot** control what goes on in the world around you.*

And you have no more than tentative and tenuous control over how you perform your life at any moment.

And you have this control only for the purpose of developing the habits that will control how you evolve in all the days ahead.

Sir Laurens Van der Post wrote mostly about his native Africa. But he was an astute observer of life. He wrote, in *Venture to the Interior:*

> *"Life is its own journey, presupposes its own change and movement, and one tries to arrest them at one's eternal peril."*

If this reminds you of Machiavelli's comments about undertaking change, it should. What Van der Post is attempting to remind us of is that the forces of things evolving out of themselves become more potent and irresistible the longer they exist. You evolve out of who you are. The older you get the more difficult and dangerous the process becomes.

You are going up against forces that want to continue on their own path. If you would change yourself in any significant way—even if it is deemed necessary to do so—would require forces for change on your part greater than the impersonal forces intending to continue you to evolve as you are. In short, becoming who you are is more powerful than becoming who you might choose to be.

The eternal peril part of it is not so easy to decode. We can't know exactly what Sir Laurens meant. But our most useful interpretation here would be that if you undertake to change, and you fail because you couldn't implement the change, you may have a worse life than you otherwise would have had. Or there is this conclusion:

> *There is no possible advantage to be gained by simply understanding the difficulty of doing life your way.*

Or,

> *Don't undertake changing the way you do life unless you have whatever it takes to complete the project.*

Both perspectives are useful—perhaps even vitally so.

Any idea that has outlasted its purpose is either excess baggage, or dangerous excess baggage. Claude Bernard, the 19th-century French physiologist who made many important discoveries, offered this observation in the Introduction to his *Study of Experimental Medicine:*

> *"Our ideas are only intellectual instruments which we use to break into phenomena; we must change them when they have* served *their purposes . . . ."*

There are two things that are very useful about this observation:

- One is that we carry around in our minds all sorts of ideas that may not be useful. This is increasingly so in our world of information overload. We assume that our carrying capacity is infinite. It is not. If you want or need a better idea, you may have to destroy one that has long since outlived its purpose. As the poet/philosopher Kenneth Burke was fond of saying, "*No construction without destruction.*" If you have habits that do not serve your purposes, you have to destroy them if you aim to replace them.

- An idea is a tool. It is not a verity. Different ideas permit different kinds of breaking-into. You want the most useful tool, not the one that is true. As Bernard knew, all knowledge—all ideas—are provisional. They have a purpose. When they have served their purpose they should be replaced, like (as he says) a lancet that has gone blunt from use.

Useless tools are excess baggage, taking up valuable space in your mind. Ideas that have outlasted their usefulness through use should be replaced (like a dull lancet). An idea may not be relevant to the circumstances. It is not just excess baggage. It is dangerous baggage.

Stasis

There is always the impetus for change—to evolve. As the 5th-century (B. C.) Heraclitus said, according to Laertius and to Plato:

"Nothing endures but change."

There is always also the opposite impetus—to keep things as they are inadvertently or not—to perpetuate the status quo. You may not want change (as in love or success), but it will happen whether you want it or not.

You may want to change, you may want to make changes in others or in the rest of the world. But the forces of stasis—of things remaining as they are—will resist you.

It isn't so much that people resist change, as the media often present it. It is simply that people are likely to prefer the familiar over the unknown. We all have our comfort zones—mentally, emotionally, and physically. It's easier and less risky to keep things the way they are.

Sometimes people want you to change. Or you may want someone else you know to change. But they are who they are because you are who you are. If that changes, who are we going to be? There is the title of a contemporary play that captures this illogic: *"I Love You, You're Perfect, Now Change."*

That's no more insane than when you fall in love with another person, and after a while be whacked on the side of the head by the fact that the reality doesn't match the fantasy image you had of the other person. The image (the mental and emotional picture you have of the other person) has staying power. Until the felt need to change to bring it into sync with the reality kicks in. Then you have a tiny exemplar of how that struggle goes on all the time in the larger world,

The twentieth-century poet Jarrell Randall laid this provocation before us (in *The Woman at the Washington Zoo*):

> *"You know what I was,*
> *You see what I am: change me, change me!"*

That may be the wish. But it can't be done. Even when necessary, we can't seem to change ourselves. Others may wish to change. But they don't do so. And *you do not have the power to make it happen*. It's been tried for centuries by people just as smart and as influential as you are. You cannot change people, even for their own good.

Twenty-five centuries ago, the ancient Greeks believed this:

> *"You cannot confer a benefit on an unwilling person."*

Nor, we might add, on a person who can't or won't understand. Why did they believe this, and we do not?

Even if the person is willing, they must be capable of making the change suggested or required. If they cannot, the effort on your part is wasted. Hector is the protagonist in Francois Lelord's novel, *Hector and the Search for Happiness*. Hector is a psychiatrist. He decides to go on a expedition around the world to seek out the real causes of happiness and unhappiness. After years of study and practice, what brought him to this life-changing juncture was that he was dissatisfied . . .

> *",,,because he could see perfectly well that he couldn't*
> *make people happy."*

Even with all of the powerful drugs at his command, and even if those people paid him for trying to change them for the better, he could not do so.

Both sociologists—Robert S. and Helen Merrell Lynd—published an influential book in 1929 based on their research, *Middletown*. In it, they wrote:

> *"It is characteristic of mankind to make as little adjustment as possible in customary ways in the face of new conditions; the process of social change is epitomized in the fact that the first Packard car body delivered to the manufacturer had a whipstock on the dashboard."*

Familiar ways, customary ways, sometimes change very slowly. New ideas like Copernicus's, and new technologies, require accommodation on the part of those who would use them. The whipstock was a standard accessory on horse-drawn buggies. Old habits and routines often die out slowly. This is not conscious resistance as such. Many are the impersonal forces of *stasis* that are always in opposition to change.

At mid-life, try changing your handwriting, or the routines you employ in driving, and your taste in wine. It is the rituals of our days that enable us to think of ourselves as still being who we are. *To abandon them would be tantamount to abandoning oneself.* Not a comfortable prospect.

The eminent British statesman Lucius Cary (in 1641) offered a provocative observation:

> *"When it is not necessary to change, it is necessary not to change."*

The operative term here is *necessary*. When *is* it necessary to change? There is always a lot of rhetoric swarming about in the media and in politics about the need to change things. Those who lead nations are wont to say that the nation needs to change to keep up.

It is certainly the case that things are always changing. Maybe we have to keep up. Yet in doing so we add impetus to the need for change. Maybe things are changing too fast. Maybe the accelerating speed of things is not good for the human condition. It certainly appears not to be good for our mental and physical health. We hurry, hurry, hurry in order to arrive at a slow death because our medical technologies can prolong our lives when those lives are no longer useful to the society. Is that the fate we aim for?

There is in addition the old saw about "keeping up with the Joneses." We are bombarded with commercials about the newest and the best. We feel inclined to keep in step with the people around us. But is the latest thing what we *need*?

In other words, how much of this constant changing is really *necessary*? And in what sense is it necessary? There is always a better mousetrap, even an anti-aging drug. Why should people who have abdicated their relevance to society burden those who are relevant to society? Is life really to be found in what is fashionable—whether it is a way of thinking, a way of home décor, or a way of putting on one's public face?

Is unbounded progress really *necessary*? Is killing the old thing the best way of getting a new thing?

When is it necessary *not to* change?

We tossed out our traditional ways because we wanted to be modern. We change our wardrobes because we want to be in fashion. We change our beliefs in keeping with the latest expert opimioms. Was what we had all that wrong?

If doing life is just a matter of keeping up, of changing with the crowd, all you have to do is let go and float downstream until you check out. You don't have to think about what would constitute a right life. All you have to do is adopt the latest fashions. At least that's the way our commercial media see it.

We lose ourselves in our effort to be in the "in" crowd.

When change is only about change, it is merely the manic delusion of the crowd.

If you would do life the way *you* would have it done, you have to know when it is necessary *not to* change. If you are one of those rare individuals who want to make well-informed choices about doing life, you have to know when it is *necessary* to change and when it is necessary *not to* change.

There is no amateur recipe for this. It requires wisdom. If you would do life the way *you* ought to do life, go forth and get wisdom. Nothing else illuminates the way: not facts, not information, not knowledge. It requires these, but more than these. It requires wisdom. You have to be able to *think* in order to do life as you would have it done. And you have to have a clear picture of where you are going and why.

And you have to know when it is necessary to change your ways, and when it is necessary not to change. That's not easy. But it is achievable. You first have to stop being a victim of change for change's sake, or for the sake of being liked by others who are solely on your screen for no other reason.

Count Leo Tolstoy is famous for many reasons, not the least of which are his quasi-philosophical novels—*War and Peace,* and *Anna Karenina.* He has always been very quotable. For a man who had thirteen children, he was a prodigious writer and thinker.

Even though, as Siddhartha is given to say, "Wisdom is not communicable," Tolstoy could be a rich source for those who might seek it anyway. Don't worry. Wisdom is probably found in the *pursuit* of it, not as a destination.

Here, we can be satisfied with the following useful observation from this philosophical writer:

> *"Everyone thinks of changing the world, but no one thinks of changing himself."*

This is not exactly true. The no one is perhaps a rhetorical exaggeration. But it still opens up some useful perspectives:

- One is that the people who most need to change themselves have probably despaired of that possibility and think instead that the solution to their problems is to change the world. This would certainly be true of most people.

- Another is that the people who are most fanatical about changing the world seem to have no clue as to how to do it—just to change it to suit them a little better personally. They will support anyone who promises to fix the world but leave them to be free.

- A third perspective is that changing the world may be good for one (or some) but bad for others. The changes that individuals yearn for are not necessarily good for the society, and vice versa.

- A fourth is that changing oneself does change the world—as Gandhi once remarked, "*You must be the change you wish to see in the world.*" Changing oneself requires others either to accommodate those changes or to excommunicate the changeling. People who try to improve their lot in life don't have as many friends as those who don't try. Have you noticed?

And of course what that implies is that the world is not going to help you change. As Gandhi said, you will be made to suffer even for trying.

So the impersonal forces of stasis (or changelessness) can be even more powerful than the forces of change.

When Dwight Eisenhower made his now-famous offhand remark, "*Things are more like they are now than they have ever been before,*" most of those who were privy to it considered it merely a gaffe. It may have been. But knowing *General* Eisenhower, it's likely he had something in mind.

Why is it that things do seem "more like they are now than they have ever been before"?

It is because the present is more real to us than either the past or the future. Before changes occur, things are only imagined. When the changes have been made, the results are visibly tangible.

Doing life is an idea. It is not until the idea is made real in the outside world that it has imperatives of its own. If you don't have the idea, there is no necessity to carry it out. If you don't have the means of carrying it out, you can't fulfill your idea.

Changes require us to accommodate to them in some way. The absence of change requires nothing of us. Change calls for our attention. The more of it there is, the more fragmented is our attention. The changes involved in becoming more of who we are have no necessary advantage to us or to others.

It is purposeful change that can matter to us and to the world in which we have to do our lives. Change that is chosen for good reasons may be of benefit, in the same way that refusing to change for good reasons may be of benefit.

Evolve, we will. But in the right direction?

The changes that are required to put us on or keep us on the right trajectory are the ones to be valued. But what is the right trajectory?

Like changelessness or stasis, change is a drug. It can be addictive, one way or the other. You have to start with your aims, and then select the changes (or the stasis) required.

Don't settle for whatever comes your way. Decide your destiny and how you have to change to pursue it. Decide what kind of other people could enable you to do life as you would.

Therein lie the changes or the retention of the values and attitude you need. You have to be a warrior to go up against the arbitrary forces (the dragons of the contemporary world you inhabit) that will otherwise victimize you.

To better quote Gandhi,

"*You must be the change you wish to see in the world.*"

If you want to change the world, first change yourself.

The world is the sum total and the consequences of the beliefs and actions of all of those who came before you, but could not or would not change. Your contribution is your contribution.

As the Nobel-Prize winner Andre Gide remarked:

"It is better to be hated for what you are than loved for what you are not."

When hypocrisy becomes the conventional way of life, the hidden costs mount like compound interest.

V

. . . Risk and Security

"Shop for security over happiness and you buy it, at that price."

—Author Richard Bach

Security is expensive. Risk is expensive. It is in the right balance between the two that a right life emerges.

Too much security diminishes life. You need only observe wild animals in the security of a zoo, or couch potatoes who have more of everything than they need. A risk-free environment (physically, mentally, or emotionally) promotes apathy and atrophy.

Too little security is like too little predictability. It is the source of angst and anguish. If you don't know where your next meal is coming from, your sense of self and of an orderly world suffer. You become disoriented.

Too much risk consumes too much of one's vital resources. You begin to lose your ability to think. Your internal GPS system goes out of whack. Your stomach is not working as it should.

Too little risk comes from too much security, and too little security leads to too much risk. The two are intimately related.

When you are growing up, you have to learn fast to avoid the social risks involved if you don't. After people get older they stop learning because they assume they know enough to be secure as long as they can fend off any serious challenges to who they are, what they believe, or how they comport themselves with their familiars. Young people are in a rush to get into their future. Older people are more likely to be content with living in their past.

People whose *lives* are actually at risk—firefighters, mountain-climbers, sky divers, combat pilots, and soldiers—report that they never felt more alive than during the most live-or-die moments. Even people whose medical prognosis is imminent death seem to come more alive.

This speaks to the paradoxical nature of both risk and security (or certainty). Americans are into welfare and avoiding risk. Both seem to diminish life—or being fully alive. We're okay with taking risks if they are guaranteed safe. The newer the roller-coaster, the more safety features it has.

We like getting a regular check because we deserve it, not because we made our contribution to the society. We want someone to protect us from harm, and even from ourselves. We want to do what we want to do, expecting someone else to take care of any bad consequences. We seem to be far less interested in prevention than with cure. Our pharmacy grows apace, alongside the cost of health care generally. We buy insurance to provide the illusion of reducing risk.

Being alive has inherent risks. Those won't go away. We just want to make them invisible.

The British clergyman and historian Thomas Fuller wrote in the 17th-century:

"He that is too secure is not safe."

What could he have meant by that?—except that there is as much danger in security as there is in risk.

The noted feminist Germaine Greer put it in even stronger terms, in 1970:

"Security is when everything is settled, when nothing can happen to you: security is the denial of life."

She probably meant security for security's sake—as an inadvertent ideology. A certain amount of security is necessary for the perpetuation of life. But risk-aversion taken too far—can indeed be the denial of life. It takes the life out of life.

The safer our comfort zones, the less life we experience. We may play games on the golf course, in the card room, or in the bedroom. But a serious look at what we consume on television is more likely to be the portrayal of life and death. It is our escape from the humdrumness of our own lives. We take risks vicariously out of some inner need to be exposed to them. What we deny in our own lives we seek to find dramatized in 3-D in the movies.

Spouses and family members may fight and argue heatedly amongst themselves. In the Western industrialized world generally, people lead very mundane existences. We try to escape the dullness of our lives through affairs, for example. But we do so in any way we can, and in any way we can afford to. We typically prefer security over risk, for which we pay heavily, and then try to add real or vicarious risk to our lives, for which we also pay heavily.

It is now deeply embedded in our culture, in our civilization. We put our environment at risk, in the name of our own security. We put our own destinies at risk, in favor of present securities. When you have too much security, you no longer contemplate the *consequences* of what you are doing but only the *means* of doing so.

In that sense, as well, security can become the denial of life.

H. L. Mencken once remarked,

> *"Most people want security in this world, not liberty."*

Isn't that because real security can be paid for only by great initial risk, and then only by eternal vigilance?

Doing life as you would have it done involves risks. If you don't know what those risks are, you may fail—or, far worse, you may give up.

Learning

There is first and universally the risks involved in learning itself. The risks are inherent in being open to the changes learning brings, as well as in the content.

You may recall this pithy characterization:

Learning = Growth, and Growth = Life

When you are habitually in the learning mode, you are always growing. Your understanding grows, your feelings grow, your mental models change and grow, and your worldview grows. Life is mainly in the process of growing, whatever part of you is involved.

The more you are in the growth mode (particularly mentally), the more alive you are and feel. The more life others perceive you to have.

But here's the risk: those around you are more likely to be in the stasis mode—much preferring things to stay as they are. If you grow, you become estranged or at odds with them. When you grow, you change. And if the world around you—or the people around you—cannot accommodate those changes, you are the enemy of the status quo.

When one spouse grows but the other doesn't, you will have problems. When the next generation is growing and yours is standing still, there will be problems. When you outwit the person who used to outwit you, you will have problems.

So there is risk involved in learning. Not only will you likely have problems with others, but you will have a problem with your earlier self.

The iconoclastic psychiatrist Thomas Szasz, whom we have met earlier, considered this a fundamental issue in *The Second Sin* (1973):

> *"Every act of conscious learning requires the willingness*
> *to suffer an injury to one's self-esteem. That is why young*
> *children, before they are aware of their own self-importance,*
> *learn so easily; and why older persons, especially if vain*
> *or important, cannot learn at all."*

Learning involves change. And in addition to risk, change involves loss—the loss of one's previous identity or sense of self. So here again is the conflict between change and stasis, in this case between becoming someone different and remaining who one has always been. How tenaciously we feel we may need to hang on to who we have *always been* is the key factor in our openness to learning.

Babies are dependent on the attentions of adults. Parents are all-powerful and largely all-controlling. Teenagers are sometimes struggling to escape the memories of that controlling relationship. This can create a problem for the parent, and for the offspring. As young people come of age, the conflicts between them and their elders is the stuff of folklore and of literature.

Learning involves such risks. You can't be sure exactly who you are going to become when you are changing. You can't be sure other people will accept you when you are no longer who you were. The safest path is to avoid any growth as a result of learning and keep the friends and endorsers you have.

But the problem then is that in taking that path you may miss out on the life that would have been engendered in risk and growth.

Doing life as you would have it done is not a matter of seeking to balance on the horns of this dilemma. It is a matter of committing to who you intend to be become and sticking to that path. There is a cost involved both in doing and not-doing. There is no path that does not have consequences.

If someone asked you to guess what period of history the following quotation came from,

> *"In ancient times, men learned with a view to their own improvement. Nowadays, men learn with a view to the approbation of others,"*

what would you say? It sounds very contemporary, doesn't it? It sounds consistent with David Riesman's 20th-century notion of being "other-directed," doesn't it?

But if you guessed the 5th-century B.C. Confucius, you would be right. His sense of things—that people were turning into the objects of others' approval (or not)—existed long before before Riesman was born.

What's interesting is how Confucius ties it into learning. Is the motive for our learning that of improving ourselves, or of gaining more status and relevance in the world? Obviously Confucius thought that made a difference. It does. If we learn only for the approbation of others, we become their victims.

Do you learn to get a better grade from the teacher or your future bosses? Or do you learn to become a more competent person, capable of making a far better individual contribution to the society? You grow either way. You gain more life either way. But to what end?

> *"Learning is like rowing upstream, not to advance is to drop back."* (Chinese saying)

> *Advance? To what end? Approbation or contribution? Via activity or accomplishment?*

Relationships

Any relationship you have with others—or with an idea or a possession—may offer a sense of comfort or security. But it also increases your risks.

As has often been observed throughout history, it is only those you trust, only those who are closest to you, who can betray you. Relationships can provide you a feeling of security. But they carry several kinds of risks.

For example, if you forge a relationship with anyone, you must now share some part of your life (and vice versa) with that other person. The path you will take in *any* relationship is *never* the path that you would take on your own. A relationship with person A—or idea X or possession Z—*never* has the same consequences as would a relationship with person B—or idea F or possession Q.

If you convince yourself (and others) that you are a liberal, you will never fully understand conservatives (and vice versa). If you drive a BMW for the image you believe it provides you, you will be reticent to drive a Dodge. If you have an exclusive friend or confidante G, you cannot have the same relationship with K.

Most murders involve people who know each other—usually well.

If you adhere to an exclusive relationship with one—supposedly as in marriage—you will find it very unnerving to try to have the same kind of relationship with another at the same time.

What returning combat soldiers find most painful is how their fellow-Americans put themselves individually first, and the community second or even last. They were vitally related to their squad, and their duty to one another came before their self-indulgences.

Relationships change everything. A vital friend in school can easily take precedence over parents—and can make a difference in how one performs in school and comports oneself in and out of school. If you read for ideas about doing life and not doing life, your relationship with the same book will be different from the reading done for an assignment—or for escape.

It could not have escaped your attention that artists prefer the company of artists, thrill-seekers prefer the company of thrill-seekers, uneducated people prefer the company of uneducated people, and thugs prefer the company of thugs. Politicians of course prefer the company of politicians and not the company of their constituents. Constituents seem to have their own interests and agendas that they want to be considered before yours.

Relationships change your tastes, your thinking, your feelings, and what you do and where you go. They change you from the outside in.

Any relationship has as its risks:

- Providing you with a feeling of security in exchange for whatever changes of direction may be required of you.

- Holding you accountable for the relationship even though you are just a part of it.

- Forming you in ways that may serve you poorly or not at all.

- Complicating your life. You now have to think—what would the other person think? For what will others' endorsers hold you accountable, with or without your knowledge?

- If you depend upon it and it fails, you fail. How much of your happiness—and sorrow—depends upon your relationships with others?

- It's easier to mistreat and to be mistreated by others who know you and your foibles well.

- A relationship not based upon common cause will inevitably lead to problems and troubles.

- Some people think that *caring* is offering unconditional love. It is not. It is refusing to let another default him or her self. Those who offer you their unconditional love are your enemies, not your enablers. You need someone to make you do what you ought to do. That's what real caring is all about.

- Whether they are intellectual, emotional, or financial, relationships are entanglements. They need to be the most strategized decisions in your life.

- Close relationships? Familiarity breeds indifference if not contempt. You can bet on it. An unquestioned belief grows stale. It will fail you, sooner or later. Fashions in everything change. If your relationships are nurtured only by the status quo, you will be out and not in. (This could be a good thing if you've thought it through.)

- A relationship you do not have cannot be used to betray you.

Relationships provide us with feelings of security. But they have many and varied risks. Like much of life, there is always a price to be paid. Nothing with others is free.

Doing life as you would have it done does not emanate from avoiding relationships—or making or keeping them. It depends upon where they will take you. If they will take you in the right direction, they are valuable. If they don't, they are harmful.

Choose wisely. When relationships no longer serve your best and worthiest purposes, discard them—especially those that feed off of misguided values and beliefs that take you down the wrong path.

Interpretations/Meanings

"Life is not meaningful . . . unless it is serving an end beyond itself, unless it is of value to someone else."
—Abraham Joshua Heschel

It may seem like a small thing—even insignificant. But it is huge in its consequences. We are busy interpreting things every waking moment of every day.

As humans, almost nothing comes our way bearing its meaning. Maybe internal distress (which we even have to learn how to interpret and express), and perhaps some external dangers come hard-wired. Being human requires that we have to learn how to interpret ourselves and our worlds. We do this by explaining things to ourselves and each other. We literally create and maintain the conscious worlds we inhabit by how we create and explain things—by how we interpret what is going on.

We live (mentally and emotionally) in a world that has been explained to us, and which we in turn explain. We have no choice but to rely on the interpretations that have been passed down to us, or to invent interpretations of our own. The things and events of the world do not participate in these interpretations. Only our words and other forms of expression do.

Mentally and emotionally, we inhabit a world made up of what we can say about it.

We usually don't even know we are doing this. It is only when our communication is problematic that we pause momentarily to consider how consequential it is.

The relevant point here however is this:

> As you communicate—as you interpret and express the
> worlds that you inhabit—you establish and maintain
> the trajectory of your life.
>
> In short, as you communicate, so shall you be.

The life of our planet may come and go, in cosmic time of millions of years. But your own life is infinitesimally shorter. You can think back and you can think forward. You can do this because you were forced or seduced into having a mind for doing so.

The minds that we have are humanly-made and maintained. They are not a part of the natural world. We have to learn how to interpret what is going on around us. And we have to learn how to express what is going on with us.

We do so by imposing *meanings* on what we want to think about or talk about. Those meanings are primarily those that are shared by the people we share them with.

That's the process. *How* we interpret things—the meanings we impose on anything and everything we want to think about or talk about—is what produces the consequences. This is so ubiquitous and so automatic that we rarely consider the fact that how we talk about things determines our destiny—both collectively and individually.

How you communicate, in this sense, determines who you will be. How you interpret things—the meaning you impose on things—determines who you are and what you can and will become.

So it makes a great difference—these simple little unconscious everyday acts. They can make a great difference.

Abraham Heschel was a contemporary philosopher of religion. He will live on in his writings as one of the most astute philosophers of our time. What he said (above) is that *life is not* (fully) *meaningful unless it is lived for a purpose beyond itself.*

American pop culture seems to be headed in the opposite direction—focusing increasingly on the individual and his or her wants and interests of the moment. Our purposes—if any—seem to have shrunk to the size of the individual. We are a consumer and entertainment society. We will eventually have more golf courses and lawns than pastures. The meat that we eat already comes mainly from crowded feed-lots.

Finding a purpose beyond oneself is becoming increasingly difficult to do. We are secular. We are anti-intellectual. We are increasingly illiterate. If people wanted to have a purpose beyond themselves, what would it be? And where is to be found the support group for such a renegade way of life?

This doesn't mean it can't be done. And one might be inclined to choose a personal rather than a collective purpose (of which there are fewer and fewer possibilities). The statesman/philosopher John W. Gardner wrote in his book *On Leadership* about his initiative Common Cause (an initiative to gather hidden [citizen] constituencies to press for more government accountability):

> *"It is virtually impossible to exercise leadership if shared values have disintegrated."*

This means that renewing American ideals rests on the shoulders of individuals, of families, of schools, and of the few actual communities remaining.

That *purpose beyond oneself* might therefore be that of renewing those ideals one person at a time. When it becomes the overriding value for children to enrich the family, and for students to be accountable for what they contribute to the classroom, the trend toward disintegration of ideals and values could be halted.

If this is the path for creating a meaningful life—surely a condition of doing life—then

Of what values and ideals will you be the exemplar
in the process of doing your own life?

Something to ponder. If a meaningful life requires doing life for purposes beyond yourself—and history leaves no doubt of this imperative—then in our present culture this may hinge upon what values and ideals *you* exemplify.

You *can* influence others by how you do life, and by how you raise your children, and by who you *are.*

This begins with how you think. For as you think, so shall you *be.* And as you are, so shall you *do.*

Doing life is not a bag of tricks. Your purposes must be beyond yourself.

In his book, *Why the Reckless Survive,* author Melvin Konner wrote:

"I sometimes think that the more reckless among us
may have something to teach the careful about the
sort of immortality that comes from living fully every
day."

One final perspective: Those who take the right risks for the right reasons (not foolishly) do so because they see the risks as worth the reward. They have a different view of immortality. To them it is not the length of life but the richness of the one you have. Yet they survive, at about the same rate as the rest of us.

What would you have all of that mean to you, as you engage in doing life?

How you interpret all of the above—what you can make it *mean* to you—will bear upon the way you go about *doing life* from this point on.

VI

. . . Belief and Belonging

To understand, you must believe.

(A variation on St. Augustine, 5th-century A.D.)

*"If you want to know what to believe, find out
what is the current consensus and turn it upside
down; that way you won't necessarily be right but
at least you won't inevitably be wrong. If, in
addition, you hope for a hint as to what is right,
listen to those whom society stigmatizes as
abnormal. They've got something."*

(David Martin writing on R. D. Laing, 1971)

What we believe is a tangled web. It is a tangled web driven by options, by opportunities, and by serendipity. It is a mix of tradition, of myth, of folklore, of happenstance, of seduction, of superstition, of prejudice, and of need.

Most people who have lived in a society with but one belief system are altogether likely to have those beliefs. The native American Indian and the Australian Aborigine would be good examples.

People who are raised in the context of strict beliefs, if cut off from contacts with other cultures, are likely to stick with those beliefs. The Amish, the Muslim, and orthodox Jewry would be good examples.

But in the modern Western world of many options, people are likely to take them—as Yogi Berra once wryly remarked.

There is one more condition. We have met this before. Traditional societies, which are likely to have far less diversity of beliefs, are typically *truth-keeping* societies. They hand down their sacred truths from generation to generation.

Modern Western societies are *truth-seeking* societies. We are in constant pursuit of the "truth." We believe therefore in progress. Innovation is good. What is newest—whether a product or a theory—is also believed to be better than what existed previously.

Thus the central paradox of modern times is that we must make things obsolete in order to trade-up, to improve, to get the latest things, to progress. Our truths are therefore provisional. They can exist only until a better one (or a more desirable one) comes along, whether that is a spouse, a detergent, a car, or a scientific theory.

That is Martin's point above, when he implies that if you stick to the consensual belief, you will always and *inevitably* be wrong—simply because any consensual idea or belief will sooner or later be displaced by what people in consensus take to be a better-because-more-recent one.

You won't necessarily be right if you choose the opposite of the consensus. But you are sure to be wrong if you choose the most popular beliefs. They are always in some state of being made obsolete by newer—and therefore supposedly better—beliefs.

Look at what was in fashion 50 years ago—whether it was a bathing suit, an automobile, or the then-current slang (which is no more than an attempt to be "with it"). The times they are a-changin'. If you are not, you will be out-of-date, a fuddy-duddy, a believer in a time past that is now obsolete. This makes you obsolete.

It's a cultural orientation. It's a cultural mindset. But it is also a paradox. Beliefs with no option may indeed seem tyrannical to us. But it won't seem tyrannical to someone who can't imagine an alternative. If you can imagine an alternative—infinite alternatives—that is also a form of tyranny. Like fish in the water, we can't see any alternatives to the belief systems we have collectively or personally.

If we were in Rome, we would do what the Romans do, to brush off that old saw. In America, we do what Americans do. We call it choice. But choices that "update" without end are also a form of tyranny.

Yet the most common cause of the choices we make about our beliefs is none of these. It is our need to *belong*. And it is our need to "understand" a world that has become increasingly incomprehensible because it is so fragmented and so open to choice. Belonging and understanding are inextricably related.

The variation on St. Augustine's observation offered at the head of this chapter is simple enough:

> *"To understand, you must believe."*

In our linear way of believing, we would assume this should be the other way around—that to believe, you would have to understand. Someone is obligated to provide you with that understanding if they wish you to believe. If someone says to you, "I love you," do you believe it or do you understand it? In order to understand what the person is saying, you first have to believe.

Contrary to popular opinion, beliefs do not emerge out of facts. It was Einstein who said something like, "You have to have a theory in order to know even what facts to look for. You catch facts in the nets of your theories." We'll return to this in a later chapter.

If you don't speak French, you are unlikely to understand what is said. You have to *believe* what the words are telling you in order to understand what is being said. In the same way, if you share the language of science, you can understand the theories that are fashionable today, *but only because you believe them.*

In his *Essays: Second Series* (in 1844), Ralph Waldo Emerson wrote:

> *"The universal impulse to believe . . . is the principal fact in the history of the globe."*

It may be more than an impulse. People in every society have always had a deep-seated *need* to believe in something together. Whether that is an individual need or not, we have no evidence. But it is clearly a *social* need. People had to believe in something *together* even to evolve into the kinds of humans we know.

Beliefs are at the core of the "collective mind," from which individual minds are spawned and nurtured. Just to get by on an average day, you have to believe that you are who you are, that other people are who they are, and that the world in which you exist is what it is purported to be.

That impulse Emerson wrote about actually comes from the human need to belong—to belong to *some* group, *some* clan, *some* community, *some* tribe, some circle of friends and acquaintances. In earlier years, those were formed by proximity. In more recent years, they are formed by shared media or by occupational or leisure pursuits and interests.

What have come to be called the social media (e.g., Face Book) enable the rapid creation and dissolution of networks of people having similar transitory interests. These are often people who want to have a public platform without any particular qualifications for having one. Every person can have his or her own bully pulpit.

The sheer fragmentation of such networks, and their speed, bode ill for any way of **belonging** to any community or group of permanence.

We have a deep-seated need to belong and thus to share permanent beliefs and values. That has become increasingly less possible. We celebrate the belief that every individual has a right to (is *entitled* to) his or her own values and beliefs. That hyper-individualism is perhaps an okay ideal. But in practice, it makes belonging to anything permanent less and less possible.

Marriage, for example, is no longer "'til death do us part." It is more likely until one or the other individual changes their minds along the way. One no longer has a job for life—but merely until that one becomes an economic burden. Paradoxically or not, this hyper-individualism renders people interchangeable, and therefore expendable.

About the need for *real* community, the sociologist and social observer Lewis Mumford wrote (in *The Transformation of Man* in 1956):

> *"To create organs for neighborly help and initiative,*
> *to meet face to face for personal assessment and vivid*
> *discussion, to take part in communal celebrations, not*
> *in vast anonymous masses, but in a circle of identifiable*
> *faces and persons, all these survivals of aboriginal*
> *village life are still necessary. They keep intact the*
> *close chain of sympathetic responses in which man*
> *first established himself as irrevocably human . . . ."*

There was good reason why the native American Indians typically limited their tribes to about 250 people. That many people can hold one another accountable.

- Mumford must obviously have been speaking to those in his intellectual community (preaching to the choir?) who already believed what he was saying. Otherwise, how to account for the fact that nothing really changed as a result of his many entreaties (here and in other writings)?

- This and many other examples raise the whole question of *hegemony* in social thinking and belief. Some beliefs become the dominant beliefs. Others recede or disappear altogether. Some beliefs dominate others simply because more people believe them—not because they are the right ones. Why did English become the hegemonic language in most of the world? Because the English-speaking world was the most powerful, the one that called the shots, the eight-hundred pound economic and military gorilla.

Some fashions become hegemonic. Others languish. Those may be fashions of thought, of diseases and palliatives, of feelings, of being, of doing, and of having. Who we *are* fits our hegemonic beliefs about who we ought to be.

In other words, *doing life* will always invoke the struggle with whatever is hegemonic in the culture. Whatever is hegemonic in doing life will always be more powerful than you are. Most people choose to go along with the fashions of the day. If that's the life you want to *do*, all you have to do is let go and float downstream with millions of others.

If it is not, you have to know the forces—overt and covert—that are massed against you. That is why doing life as you would have it done ranges from difficult to impossible. The hegemonic forces are bigger and more powerful than you are.

Belonging

We have the beliefs that are hegemonic in the groups, the cultures, and the subcultures we belong to. The need to belong is universal. The beliefs that come with our belonging are endemic—that is, they come with the group we belong to.

So it may make a difference—all of the difference—which group or groups we fall into or choose to belong to.

If you want to speak English, it helps to start with an English-speaking family. If you want to be musical, it helps to be brought up in a musical family. If you want to be a Muslim, it helps to be brought up in a Muslim family/community.

Early environment does not guarantee a destiny, any more than genetics does. You can't predict your future unless you take the hegemonic path. Then your future will be just like everyone else's, whatever that turns out to be. But you can, within limits, *make* your future.

The key point here is that you can change yourself as thoroughly as you choose by choosing the group or groups to belong to. *Belonging* makes certain beliefs—certain ways of doing life—necessary. To *belong*, you have to abandon the life you had for the one you want to have. Beliefs—ways of thinking, being, doing, having, and saying—are a condition of *belonging*. What they offer is what the critic and philosopher George Steiner referred to as "alternities"—alternative ways of doing life.

In all of human history, only a handful of people have done life exclusively their own way. They have belonged to the groups they needed to belong to in order to execute in their lives the beliefs they needed. Artists have usually belonged to certain groups of artists. The Impressionists had to form their own group to bolster their artistic beliefs.

Methodists talk more to those who belong as Methodists in the same way that agnostics prefer the company of agnostics. The smallest group you can belong to is a group of two. Once a marriage (for example) has been infected by a third person, it often dissolves—in spirit if not legally. You can't belong to a belief group that doesn't exist.

Beliefs are very rarely individually chosen. They are a mandate of belonging to a particular group.

Beliefs very rarely emerge in isolation. They cannot be nourished and embellished in isolation. They require continuous reinforcement.

The famous writer and source of epigrams, Montaigne, wrote (in 1580):

> *"The greatest thing in the world is to know how to belong to oneself."*

Great in part, perhaps, because knowing how to belong to oneself is so rare. It is possible, of course, to imagine being a community of one—as did Gandhi. But that requires a strength of will most people cannot muster.

Better to choose the groups to belong to that require the beliefs which will further your own interests in doing your own life.

With loss of community goes loss of genuine belief. Loved ones constitute a sort of community. We belong to them, and they belong to us. With the loss of that sense of belonging goes the beliefs on which it is based. Most of us have experienced that bewildering sense of loss. We can no longer belong. We can no longer believe in what we believed in.

There is something similar on a larger scale. The poet Walt Whitman—of *Song of Myself* fame—wrote of his disillusionment in *Democratic Vistas* (in 1871):

> *"Never was there, perhaps, more hollowness of heart than at present, and here in the United States. Genuine belief seems to have left us."*

If you want genuine belief, there has to be genuine belonging. It was the inevitable disintegration of community in a growing democracy he was witnessing. In a democracy, there are no longer people you know personally, only votes. There are no beliefs beyond entitlements. Democracy is supposed to make us equal. It does not. It differentiates us even more than before along the lines of status, of the hierarchy of fashion and money. We believe in haves and have-nots.

There is no overarching belief in anything that does not affect us directly. We believe in radical individualism. That pervades our culture. We have no common cause, no genuine beliefs about where we are going as a civilization, as a society. That's because we are not a group but a splintering of individuals, all wanting what *they* want, with little or no concern for the consequences.

Few people seem to realize that belonging and belief are the parents of life—of being human.

Those who aim to do life independently of *what* they belong to suffer the fate of the blind leading the blind. We teach people what they ought to want. But we no longer try to teach them to want what they *should* want.

We have come to put on and take off our beliefs for the impression they might make on those who observe us. We regale ourselves for posing. Our beliefs, like much else about us, have become commodities that can be bought and sold.

We have more and know more than any people who have ever lived on this earth. But we're not certain what any of it *means*. We no longer have the genuine beliefs that enable us to discriminate. A person who has a specific aim in life therefore has an advantage. There is less competition on *that* path. If you commit to a cause for your life, you have a basis for making what's relevant meaningful, and for making irrelevant what's not.

If something belongs to you, you belong to it. If someone belongs to you, you belong to that person. If an idea belongs to you, you belong to it. If you belong to a group (whatever the beliefs and orientations shared), it belongs to you. If you do not further its interests, you cannot belong.

Belonging demands its price. People may get frustrated, but there is no free belonging. If you are an American or a citizen of any other country, you are obligated to make your contribution to the health and welfare of the country to which you belong. As JFK said, "Ask not what your country can do for you; ask what you can do for your country."

That was obviously rhetorical. That's not how most American citizens think. The thought didn't even originate with JFK. It originated with Oliver Wendell Holmes, Jr.

Native American Indians not only believed it. They enforced it. The freedom to do whatever they wanted didn't begin until after they had made their contribution to the tribe by performing their roles in an exemplary fashion. If we really believed it, it would be a condition of belonging as a member of this country.

Any belonging that does not have mutual obligations is dysfunctional—whether in a family, a friendship, a marriage, or any other collective. For example, a person who is a member of any kind of organization has at least a moral obligation to make that organization healthy if he or she expects a healthy return. A poorly-performing organization in the real world cannot be expected to support its people without first having their superior contributions.

When entitlements outpace contributions, the organization sickens and dies. A dysfunctional family has its priorities wrong. It's not what the members of that family feel entitled to because they belong to it. It is first what they contribute to the health and welfare of that family. *Belonging* that pays off has an up-front and continuing price.

The French philosopher, novelist, playwright, and critic Jean-Paul Sartre (who declined a Nobel Prize) wrote in *Words*, his autobiography:

> *"I confused things with their names: that is belief."*

To believe in the idea or the image or the concept of something, and not that something as such . . . is belief.

To be in love you must believe you are in love. Even then, you will be in love with the image you carry of your loved one—not the person as such.

Problems arise when the reality challenges the belief. To accept history as a true story of the past is to believe what you believe. To know your past, you must believe it. To make your future, you must believe in yourself *there*—not in those who purport to foretell your future.

To communicate with one another, we must pretend that the name for something is the same as the real thing. We cannot put the real things in our minds—only the names and images for them. Ancient people believed their legends before they believed the facts. Our facts, a maypole for modern life, have displaced our beliefs about ourselves and our worlds.

We believe in the illusion of our facts. Ancients believed in the illusion of their fables. Both ways are possible. Which is the way that better serves human and social ends? There are no *facts* in love or faith or hope.

We live by and in our beliefs—whether those beliefs support science or mythology. Take away the feelings, and there are no facts about love, or hate, or freedom.

Do the names of things precede the existence of things? Or is it the other way around? Quarks were not observed before there was a name for them. Do you or I exist apart from what we believe and are believed to *be*?

Doing life, therefore, probably requires first the creation of a myth or an illusion. You have to begin there. Then of making it a belief held by others to whom we *belong* and who *belong* to us. If there is a short-cut, it has yet to be invented.

What is *believable* to people depends upon what those people—or you—already believe. What you *can* believe depends upon what you already believe.

In your journey from infancy to adulthood, you belonged to many people, to many ideas, to many things. Every belonging added to the beliefs you already harbored. Linus has his blanket, which became a part of our perception of him.

What did you have that became a part of who you are, as others thought of you and therefore as you thought of yourself?

Our illusion is that we believe in the facts of the world. We don't. We believe in our beliefs about whatever we encounter in our lives. Black holes may fascinate astrophysicists. But they are not very relevant to an unemployed receptionist.

We concern ourselves with what is *relevant* to us. And what is relevant to us is a function of how we interpret the world. We interpret our world according to our beliefs about it. If we belong—in part—to our jobs and to the organization that issues our paychecks and we don't have one of those, how can we belong to what we no longer have?

Our beliefs—long-term or transient—dictate what is relevant and what is not. What is relevant to us is what that something *means*. And that something *means* whatever our beliefs determine it to mean.

Your mind describes and defines your world for you.

*How you think—because of your past and present belongings—determines who you **are**. And it is in who you **are** that lie the most probable determinants of who you can be.*

Doing the life that you desire requires that you belong to those beliefs that will make it possible. You have to change those first.

We started with a perspective from R. D. Laing. We can close with a similar perspective from Jean-Jacques Rousseau, the French political philosopher, who is best known for his book *The Social Contract,* set forth this observation in 1762:

> *"Take the course opposite to custom and you will almost always do well."*

Who would have thought that doing life as you would have it requires so much courage, so little belonging, and such contrary beliefs?

VII

. . . Habits and Intentions

*"The more one analyses people, the more all
reasons for analysis disappear. Sooner or later
one comes to that dreadful universal thing
called human nature."*

—Oscar Wilde (in *The Decay of Lying*)

And nowhere, we might add, does human nature exhibit itself more "dreadfully" than in the prevalence of habits and intentions.

A worthy intention not acted upon is a lie. Lying to oneself is like a rotting from the inside out. And we don't "have" habits. *They have us.* We have no choice but to follow where our habits lead us.

Enchained, we follow where our habits lead us unless, of course, we displace the wrong ones with the right ones. But then we would have to be able to distinguish between the ones we have and the ones we need. What would a habit of being able to do that look like and feel like to us before we made it a part of who we are?

The Swiss academician and author Henri Amiel, best known for his posthumous *Journal Intime (19th-century)* made this incisive observation:

*"To learn new habits is everything, for it is to reach the
substance of life. Life is but a tissue of habits."*

Habits enable us to do things without thinking about them—as the philosopher Alfred North Whitehead reminded us. Thus we depend upon them for our progress. We build new capabilities atop existing habits.

Any musician or professional athlete knows how this works.

As we considered earlier, you do not simply have habits. *They have you.* They are the infrastructure of your thinking, your feelings, and your actions. You add or subtract a bit here and there. But it is your habits that determine your life. It is not your hopes or your intentions.

So the foundation for doing life as you would have it done is that of your habits. Get those right and you can live life the way you would. The Samurai (the Japanese warrior cult) practiced total discipline. How they comported themselves extended from their swordsmanship and their social and battle encounters to how they braided their hair. The Amish, like the Quakers, practice the simple habits of gardening and dish-washing in just the right way. They know that these habits are building blocks for higher habits.

We harbor in our modern pop culture the notion that freedom is freedom *from* habits and the discipline they enable. We seem not to realize that "letting it all hang out" is as much a habit as is civility. So as a people we have become less civil and more self-absorbed. You have to practice your whims in order to make them seem, well, spontaneous. This requires no less discipline than does becoming a capable jazz improviser.

Composers and innovators of every kind operate at the peak of a pyramid of established habits. The right habits enable them to think about creating at the next level.

The famous sculptor and inventor Michelangelo said that

> *"Creativity is a function of discipline."*

It was the right habits built on the right habits that enabled him to consciously create his masterpieces. Life done *right* is no less an art form than was Michelangelo's sculpture and paintings. Doing life creatively (and of real value to other people as was Michelangelo's work) requires the discipline that only right habits can provide.

This holds whether you are a president, a pipefitter, or a home-maker. If life is but "a tissue of habits," the right kind of life is built on the right kind of habits for the roles you take on, and for your expectations about doing life.

If you practice what you desire to be until the right habits take over, you mightily increase the probabilities of arriving there. If you don't, you will arrive somewhere else.

Most of your habits take over by default. Because of who you fall in with and how indiscriminately you go about feeding your mind, like most people you will end up with the habits that serve you poorly—or even negatively. What you fail to choose for yourself will be chosen for you.

The celebrated author of his famous *Dictionary* and many other writings, Samuel Johnson once quipped as follows about how habits take over without our awareness or our permission:

> *"The chains of habit are too weak to be felt until they are too strong to be broken."*

If we think something or feel something or do something repeatedly, it becomes a habit. Our driving down a familiar street is largely by habit. Driving down an unfamiliar street requires our attention. If we apply our theories about the world and how it works often enough, they become habits. The more familiar we are with another person, the more likely we are to treat that person (and be treated by that person) in habitual ways.

We have routines that we carry out in much the same way every day. These are habits. Habits, it has often been said, are hard to break. They are easy to come by. Then, unfelt and even unwelcome, they take over and we are in their thrall.

If they are not chosen for good reason, they will develop and take you over for no reason beyond simply practicing them.

Are they too strong to be broken? That way of seeing them makes it so. They become the core of who we are. We identify ourselves by our habits. They are, indeed, usually often stronger than our own wills. You are likely to lose if you face-off to them.

They may be too strong to be broken, but they can be displaced. You can weaken and finally eliminate them *only by displacing them with other chosen habits*—essentially in the same way as you got them in the first place—imperceptibly. Don't fight a habit. Betray it by a chosen habit. Practice that chosen habit and the wrong one will be eroded to extinction.

Achievers in any walk of life consciously build the pyramids of habits they need in order to achieve. Mediocre performers are had by the habits they happen to have. Achievers create, practice, and fine tune the habits they need. As the 16th-century humanist Erasmus put it:

> "A nail is driven out by another nail. Habit is overcome
> by habit."

Doing life as you would have it done requires the same level of deliberate choice and of practicing the habits you need in order for them to take you where you want to go. You can't get there without the particular habits—from the largest to the smallest—you need to take you there.

For example, if you want to be respected (use any verb) by other people, perform your role as if there were no option for those others. If you want to be loved, be a great lover. If you want to be smart, practice the difficult habits of getting there. Perform your role(s) as you desire to be perceived, and the habits driving you and others will take over.

For those who would be life-*doers* and not one of those who are *done-to* by life, there is an indispensable insight provided by the 19th-century Russian poet Alexander Pushkin:

> "Habit is Heaven's own redress;
> It takes the place of happiness."

You probably never thought of it that way—habit as a substitute for happiness. Is that possible?

As a practical matter, the more your habits control you, the less happiness you will have. The more habit-bound you are, the less happiness you will experience. This may or may not be "Heaven's own redress." But it makes sense. Habits turn you off, permit you to navigate the world without thinking about it. Happiness cannot penetrate, because it requires vulnerability, awareness, wonder, surprise.

The more routinized a love affair becomes, the less love there is in it. The joy is gone. The elation is gone. The wonder is gone. Routines take the place of the happiness that we were seeking.

The 20th-century Irish playwright and novelist Samuel Beckett understood this well. In his famous *Waiting for Godot* (1955) he wrote:

> *"The air is full of our voices. (He listens.) But habit is a great deadener."*

Routines at work put people in a semi-conscious mode. They are operating on autopilot. They are not fully engaged. We experience more happiness in leisure pursuits, because those are less routinized. We are more fully engaged. And that is what we sometimes experience as "happiness" or "fun."

It may not be important. But happiness has to occur in its own way. And the habits we develop to get us through the day (and the night) block out the conditions necessary for happiness to occur.

So there is a very provocative connection between habits and doing life. If you want fullness in life, it is best to keep habits for things that don't matter so much—like which hand you use to cut your steak or to shave.

Some people are more seductive than others. That's because they are more fully alive. Engaging yourself in life or engaging others with you requires that you do so in a non-habitual way. People are different. They will be attracted to you to the extent you engage them as being different. You can't do that if you have the habit of stereotyping others or if you stereotype yourself by being habit-bound.

If you are wearing your full self-protective armor (habits), you cannot fully engage people, or life.

Doing life requires meeting it on its terms, not yours. Habits constitute your terms, not life's.

Closely related (perhaps) is an observation that comes from Aristotle (c. 3rd-century B.C.):

> *"We are what we repeatedly do. Excellence* (or any other personal achievement) *is not an act, but a habit."*

This can be made to be very useful. We may entreaty ourselves or others to be excellent. But we are using the wrong pointer. You cannot perform excellence on the spot because it is your will to do so. It is an achievement that can only be built up over time and on top of a whole pyramid of right habits.

Our pop culture misleads us. Our capabilities are not raised by inspiration. Nor are they lowered by an indifferent world. Your performance in the world (or with yourself) is a function of the habits that do it for you—or not.

Your habits are the engine of who you are. And they are the controllers that will direct you, drone-like, into the future that those particular habits can and *must* make of you.

The well-known English poet William Wordsworth (1770-1850) offered these lines for our consideration:

> *"Not choice*
> *But habit rules the unreflecting herd."*

Probably true. But the *reflecting* few are also ruled by habits—in this case the habits that support and nurture reflection.

When people are habit-bound, they have lost their interest in—and their capability—for making choices. They do everything by habit so they do not have to make an attentive choice.

Still, when a person opts for doing life rather than being done-to *by* life, that's the first choice that has to be made. And then there are all of the other choices that have to be made to implement that choice. These are not choices about whether you want to or not. They are ultimately choices about the kinds of habits you need in order to realize the first choice—to make happen what you want to happen.

That brings us to the bugbear of . . . *intentions.*

Intentions

At one time or another, we probably all *intend* to do the right thing—to BE the right thing. And we all know that the road to hell is paved with good intentions.

An intention is merely self-deception if you haven't got what it takes (mainly the right kinds of habits) to fulfill your daydreams in the real world. Most people's intentions are indeed a form of boasting which, when believed by others, becomes a form of self-deception—of lying to oneself.

Intentions may indeed be a necessary part of learning how to do the kind of life you would choose. If used as private, unrevealed promises to oneself, they are probably not especially harmful. But if you make your intentions public and do not fulfill them, you lose confidence in yourself.

Other people don't need to know what your intentions are. They can deduce your intentions from your actions, from how you perform your life. Your intentions are implicit in your accomplishments. Otherwise, talking about them erodes them, brings them to the level of meaningless chit-chat.

Keep your intentions to yourself. Be known for your accomplishments, not your intentions.

As the columnist Evan Esar wrote:

> *"Good intentions, like good eggs, soon spoil unless they are hatched."*

Too many intentions not carried out are like landfills in the mind. They make the space unusable for anything but more trash.

A propos of what has more recently been characteristic of our own Congress, the 18th-century English writer and political commentator Horace Walpole wanted us to be fully aware of

> "... *how many more events the **faults** of statesmen give birth, than are produced by their good intentions.*"
> (emphasis mine)

Like most people, statesmen and congressional incumbents probably cause more problems than they solve. This is not because they do not have good intentions. It is because they have neither the courage nor the wherewithal to act on their good intentions. They take actions unrelated to their best intentions. They thus create consequences that have little or nothing to do with their good intentions.

They are therefore like most people. Most people do not live the lives that they profess they want. They, too, are well-intentioned. But in dealing with what they take to be the events of the day, they create consequences in their own and others' lives that are far removed from their good intentions.

Is that the "dreadful universal thing called human nature" that Oscar Wilde wrote about at the top of this chapter?

Wilde probably had good intentions in offering his epigram. So he created a provocation for us that is unrelated to his good intentions. He allowed us to overlook the fact that there are cultures in which intention plays no part. You either performed as you ought or you didn't. If you did, you live to perform another day. If you didn't, you might have been excommunicated, or worse.

In some cultures, there is no way of talking about intentions. Your intentions would have been irrelevant, not worth talking about. It was only what you achieved or failed to achieve that mattered. Did you do what you should have done? Did you refrain from doing what you should not have done?

That's really all that needs knowing, isn't it?

In our modern Western culture, having trickled down from our freedoms, intention is taken to be a key to understanding. If you didn't *intend* to kill that other person, you might be acquitted in a court of law. But what difference does that make to the person who was murdered?

In organizations, the members may affirm their intention to do the right thing. But if you sent the wrong order, how would you say the organization performed? Even CEOs have good intentions. But if they preside over the demise of the company they are leading, of what value were their intentions?

The marriage vow may be *forever*. Most newly-minted spouses have good intentions. But if the marriage goes sour, of what value were those intentions?

You see the point. An intention has worth only if it is carried out. Else it is social lubrication. And if that is what Oscar Wilde was referring to, then it is "dreadful universal human nature." At least in our culture it is.

Doing life as you would have it done requires you never to have an intention you do not act upon successfully. If you can't—or won't—fulfill an intention, it is better not to have had that intention at all.

If you cannot or do not carry out your intentions, they will serve you ill.

In our Christian Bible (Luke:14) you will find this caution:

> *"Which of you, intending to build a tower, sitteth not*
> *down first, and counteth the cost, whether he have*
> *sufficient to finish it."*

If you substitute the word "life" for the word "tower" (as it was possibly intended as this kind of metaphor), you have the indispensable rule for doing life as you would have it:

> *If you are not willing or capable to pay*
> *the price (which is whatever it takes) to*
> *do life as you would have it, then your*
> *good intentions do not matter. Admit your*
> *shortfalls and move on. Never, never*
> *commiserate the life you might have had.*
> *Make the most of what you have.*

That's the consolation prize. It is far better than a basketful of empty promises and intentions.

It is your habits that make possible and necessary the future life you will have. Your momentary intentions are just that—momentary intentions. For the most part, they have no influence over the bundles of habits of which you are made.

> *Doing life as you would have it done requires first putting together solidly the bundles of habits that can get you there. Habits that take you in some other direction must be "killed"—displaced by the habits you need. It is habits that underwrite achievement.*
>
> *It is good to have intentions, but only if they are the ones you need to do the life you would have. And then only if you bring them to fruition.*
>
> *Intentions you don't fulfill become clutter in your inner workshop. The right intentions not acted upon in the right way preclude the habits you need to maneuver yourself in the right direction.*

VIII

... Explaining and Prognosticating

"A know-it-all is always recognized by his ability to explain everything."

—Evan Esar

"The moment a person forms a theory, his imagination sees in every object only the traits which favor that theory."

—Thomas Jefferson

Explaining is a form of theorizing. We explain what something is by naming it. We explain why something happened by accounting for it in some way. We explain why things are the way they are by telling a story of how those things got to be that way. We explain ourselves to ourselves and to other people. We ask other people to explain their behavior if it doesn't fit well with what we expect.

All of these are sort of provisional theories. We create or import mental models to account for everything that occurs to us, or might occur to us. They were originally hypotheses—conjectures that seemed at the time plausible to us. Most of these we pick up from other people or from the cultures or the subcultures to which we belong—or would like to belong.

We live by beliefs. We were not born with these beliefs. For the most part, they existed before we were born. They were imposed upon us by those around us—family, friends, teachers, preachers, and increasingly by the media we consume. We see how they are construed, and become capable of making up our own beliefs—our own theories about everything inside and outside of us.

Everything that makes sense to us has implicit premises. We unwittingly use those to create more theories—our *beliefs*.

They are formulaic. They fit what we perceive to be the case. We often make them up from a single experience with a person or an event. They are thus anecdotal. As Jefferson said (above), we don't look for evidence that might contradict our beliefs/theories. We interpret the evidence to fit the belief, not the other way around.

We see the world through our explanations of it, whether those explanations are temporary or permanent (as in sacred beliefs). If you are angry with a person or a situation, you will see the world through that lense. Everything else is on hold, including your better judgment. If you like a person or a situation, you will look at that person or situation through the lenses of approbation or affection.

If you are committed to doing life as you would have it done, you have to control the lenses through which you look at a person or a happening. How you feel about the person or the happening is ultimately irrelevant. What *is* relevant is how you interpret what is going on—given what you are trying to accomplish.

People who learn how to do life as they would have it done come to recognize that how they feel about people or things is not the issue. The issue is how *strategically* they can learn to maneuver in any situation. They come to realize that they have to *de-center* themselves. What is going on is almost never the cause for how they personally react to it.

> Your personal reactions may be like shooting yourself
> in the foot. You may thereby be creating an impediment
> rather than a facilitation. You are not the judge. The "judge"
> is what you are trying to accomplish. What optimizes your
> movement in that direction is the right way to think and

to act. Any way of thinking or doing that does not move
you in that direction is an impediment.
Most people report that their initial, impulsive reactions
were wrong.
Doing life the way you would have it done has to be
deliberate, not self-indulgent. You have to see yourself
and control yourself from a distance. You have to be the
strategic director of what comes next, not the person who
compulsively or habitually simply acts out feelings.
You have to interpret things not according to you, but
according to what you are trying to accomplish.

People are compulsive about explaining things, and also about forming theories from their incidental experiences.

It seems that we are the creatures who have to explain things. Other critters don't. And some of them have been around for hundreds or thousands of years. They form hypotheses about how they managed to escape a predator, for sure. But those hypotheses are provisional. They are good only until the next encounter. If they form a habit, they are now some other critter's dinner.

Nor do they try to explain to themselves why they are being hunted, or why they are the hunter. It is enough to know how to avoid a predator or find food or a mate. Elaborate explanations are academic.

Yet most *people* engage in them compulsively. And we devour our celebrities' explanations. We say to them, "Explain me to myself."

After becoming somewhat of a celebrity expert, Charles Darwin took to explaining himself to himself (apparently because there was no "Dr. Phil" in those days). What he wrote in his *Autobiography* (in 1892) shed some light on this compulsion to theorize about everything:

> *"I have steadily endeavored to keep my mind free so as*
> *to give up any hypothesis, however much beloved (and*
> *I cannot resist forming one on every subject) as soon as*
> *facts are shown to be opposed to it."*

A noble sentiment. However, if your status in science depended upon there being no facts opposed to your hypothesis, there would be no science. When your very identity is at stake, would you abandon what you had built your public image on?

He was a poet. And poets often reveal truths of which we were unaware. We know this because if he were a bona fide researcher, he would have done this the other way around. He would have begun with the reasons why he could not possibly cling to his hypothesis, rather than waiting for someone else to provide any contrary facts.

Still, that misses the point. For where we humans are concerned, we have beliefs that are impervious to the facts. Scientists do, priests do, physicians do, auto mechanics do, and the rest of us do.

We have to believe *something*. We are not hot-wired to get by if we don't. So we come to Darwin's implicit point:

> *Whether or not a hypothesis or a theory is true or*
> *not makes little difference. If it is believed by enough*
> *people, that will make it de facto true.*
> *Doing life requires clinging to certain beliefs—like "I am*
> *who I am because that's who I am." Will such a belief*
> *get you to where you want to go?*
>
> *That is the pragmatic issue. If you don't have the kinds*
> *of theories (beliefs) that will get you where you want*
> *to go, change them to ones that do.*
> *And, as Jefferson said and Einstein echoed, you will*
> *net with your beliefs the facts you need to support*
> *those beliefs. That's how Darwin did it. If he didn't*
> *have the facts he needed, he invented them. And look*
> *how his belief has impacted thinking until this day!*

Or, as the German philosopher of history Oswald Spengler put it:

> *"The stupidity of a theory has never impeded its influence."*

It was the Nazis who were most influenced by Spengler's theory of historical determinism.

> *Progress (even in your own life) comes not from being reasonable, but being unreasonable—as G. B. Shaw professed. In other words, the more conventional your beliefs, the more conventional will be your life. If you intend to have an unconventional life, you have to be unreasonable about it.*
>
> *All theories are tools. They were invented. Invent those that serve your purposes for how you would undertake doing life. It doesn't matter if they are true or not. What matters is whether they are serving your own best self-interests or not. The culture or subculture you inhabit is not there to serve your purposes. It is there to serve its own purposes. If those are yours, then you already have the life you deserve.*
>
> *If not, then you have to invent the tools to get there.*

While you are still ruminating on George Bernard Shaw, consider this from him as a useful explanation of things:

> *"People are always blaming their circumstances for what they are. I don't believe in circumstances. The people who get on in this world are the people who get up and look for the circumstances they want, and if they don't find them, make them."*

On Prognostication

We will be using this term *prognostication* in the ordinary dictionary definition of predicting, foretelling, or prophesying. However, we will also be using it not in any abstract sense, but in the sense that this is something people do frequently every day.

For example, if you hesitate to say something to someone because you anticipate that this will make them upset if you say it, you are prognosticating. You actually don't know what is going to happen because it hasn't happened yet. You are guessing. You are predicting. You are prognosticating.

Prognostications play a critical role in everyday thinking and everyday behavior. You may not do something because of your unspoken prediction about how it might turn out if you did. To put it most simply: we predicate what we say or do on the theories we have formulated out of past experiences. But what we say or do is also determined by our beliefs about what will happen if we do say or do this or that.

To the extent that you actually think about what you are going to say or do, the two perspectives taken together is where you stand. Interpreting the present by explaining the past is the same operation as deciding on a present action by taking into account your prognostication about the consequences.

It's like being suspended in a web that extends from your imagined past into your imagined future.

So how you perform yourself in the present depends upon how you explain your past and how you foresee your future. Your habits will keep you in that web that extends from your past into your future unless you make the heroic effort to re-invent them.

Most efforts that people make to redirect their future fail because they do not see that they have to reweave the whole fabric—from the past into the future. Merely trying to change won't do it. You have to re-compose your story from your past through to your future. Then you can do what has to be done in the present.

But here we are not talking about foretelling the future. We are talking about inventing it. As we have already encountered, the best way of predicting the future (which actually can't be done) is to invent it. Inventing your future *requires re-inventing your past*. Both are highly creative. You must be the artist of your future by becoming the artist of your past.

The famous economist (who taught at Harvard for many years) John Kenneth Galbraith had something pragmatically useful to say to us:

"There are two classes of people who tell what is going to happen in the future: Those who don't know, and those who don't know they don't know."

What are we to make of this?

- First, that there are only these two kinds of people—those who don't know what is going to happen in the future, and those who don't know they don't *know* what is going to happen in the future.

- That fairly well eliminates the people who think they know what is going to happen in the future. No one does.

- Yet those who don't know what is going to happen in the future still prophesy what is going to happen in the future. These must be the experts—the people who get paid for telling what us what is going to happen in the future even though they're only prognosticating. They can be right only by happy accident.

- Then there are those who don't know they don't *know* what is going to happen in the future. That must be all the rest of us. But that does not stop us from prognosticating—about the smallest things in our lives to the largest concerns of humanity.

- People are apparently stuck between having to explain their pasts and to prognosticate their futures, and trying to work out some kind of life in the present that their story line provides them.

This is where *doing life* comes in. The life you are capable of doing depends upon how creatively you craft the story of your past through to your future. You are suspended by that story in the present, which is the only place you have for doing life.

People often fail at doing life when they do not recognize that they are in the story that stretches from their past into their future. Your story has to hang together no matter the life you work out. You might as well make it the kind of story that serves your purposes for the life you would do.

You could be the author of the story of your life rather than letting the life you happen to have be the author of you. They are both created.

> *The key question about doing life is whether or not you can learn to be capable of creating it, of writing it, of scripting it, of authoring it. If you let the happenings of the moment or of your life author your life as they will, then you cannot be doing life. It will be done to you.*

There is a sort of folkloristic notion (which is always suspect) which would have us believe that if we had enough power, we could make the future be whatever we wanted. Hitler had it, and he had a plan. Napoleon had it, and he had a plan. Cleopatra had it, and she had a plan. But no one could argue that they achieved exactly what they set out to achieve.

Alexander had it, and he had a plan. To a large extent, he achieved what he set out to achieve. But he knew how to rewrite history, not just to write history. The past and the future he invented were the key to the present he lived.

There is a Chinese saying that is as follows:

> *"To prophesy is extremely difficult—especially with respect to the future."*

Prophecy is thin stuff compared to a story that is presented as inevitable. That is what you must do if you intend to do life as you would have it done. You must live and be seen living a story that is compelling because it is made to seem inevitable—to you and to others.

The French poet and critic Paul Valery (1871-1945) wrote in his book, *The Outlook for Intelligence:*

> *"The future is endowed with **essential unpredictability**, and this is the only prediction we can make."*

That's okay. It serves to remind us that it is not about predictability in the first place. It is about creating the life you would *do* in the context of that unpredictability.

Doing life as you would have it done is not about foretelling the future. It is about creating your own future out of your own present, which you have created out of your past. It can never be perfect. We rarely live happily ever after.

But that's a red herring anyway. Doing life is not to be had in the pursuit of happiness (however you might define that). It is had in the process of continuously re-inventing yourself for your purposes in the context of whatever life throws at you. It is had in the process of incorporating the adversities of life into the story you compose about your life and for your life.

There have always been prophets of one kind or another. And there have always been what the longshoreman-turned-philosopher Eric Hoffer called "true believers." Mass movements are inspired and peopled by true believers.

True believers read about their futures provided by astrologers. It has been reported that there are more astrologers in the U. S. than there are astronomers. But there are also palm readers, tea readers, tarot cards, and dozens more tricks and techniques for foretelling your future.

Fate is probably the oldest human belief. Fatalism has endured. It is still alive and well. Whenever you begin speculating on why this or that happened—to *you*—you are engaging in fatalism. Are you culpable? Was it something you said or did, or something you didn't say or do?

You don't "find" a soul-mate. You create one. Self-fulfilling prophesies abound. You believe in something and if it comes true it was meant to be. If it doesn't, it was not meant to be that way. You win either way. That kind of circular thinking will not serve you well.

There are many people who are desperately curious about what their daily, weekly, or life's fate may be. That simply means that there are millions of people who believe in fate—and that their own can be foretold. Even Alexander the Great visited an oracle to acquire a prediction about the fate of his ambitions.

In *The Prophets (1962)*, the religious philosopher Abraham Joshua Heschel wrote:

> *"What the poets know as poetic inspiration, the prophets call divine revelation."*

Poetic inspiration amounts to a flash of insight into how to express something profound in a new and powerful way. Artists have it. Inventers have it, as Thomas Edison proved. Occasionally it may even occur to you. There is more inspiration than perspiration in deciding—intuitively—what is to be done.

Maybe Heschel is right. Maybe he is not. Who would actually know what goes on in the privacy of anyone's mind? But we will interpret it according to our beliefs about it.

We may overlook the fact that **everything** has been or has to be interpreted. What something *means* is always a human construct. There may be the same thing called by different names. There may be different things called by the same name.

Here is what's important in doing life as you would have it done:

- Don't confuse the name of something for that something. The reality and how we explain it are always two fundamentally different things.

- Don't prophesy. As someone once said, "An ounce of action is worth a ton of theory."

- The only test of your every day prognostications is how things turn out. Don't dwell on being wrong—or right. You cannot control the consequences. You cannot control what happens in the world outside of yourself (no matter how you imagine it).

- It is enough to say, "Things are the way they are because they got to be that way," and move on. The complexities of the real world are beyond the capabilities of our understanding.

The famous king Fionn of Ireland was puzzled by the perplexing actions of the white doe he was chasing. But he didn't impose his explanations on the situation. He was wise. He apparently said to himself, "I don't know why she did what she did. But I know enough not to question things that cannot be explained."

The lesson here is simple enough:

Do not impose your hypotheses on the world. Let them impose their reality on you.

We rush to explain everything. But some things cannot be explained. Perhaps there are even things that should not be explained or reduced to theory. It is enough that they are what they are.

Love may be the best example. In trying to explain or analyze everything, you may destroy its meaning for you.

The Bulgarian-born Nobel prize winner Elias Canetti wrote (1905-1994) in *The Secret Heart of the Clock*:

"Prophecy is malicious deception . . . ."

We ought not to think of this in the abstract. He is talking about something that people do frequently every day. Thus we would interpret the lesson differently: When you prognosticate, you are *maliciously deceiving* not the world—but yourself.

Pragmatically, the damage done by prognosticating is the damage done to oneself. The only way you can know whether or not you should say something or do something is after you've done it (or not) and you confront the consequences. Then you will know.

You cannot know for sure, nor can you control, the consequences of what you do or say. So you may do what Thomas Edison did. Do the right thing and see how it turns out. If you knew beforehand what the consequences were gong to be, you might get in the way of doing the right thing. You could be wrong. But how else are you going to find out for sure?

Prudence in action serves you better than prognostication in your thinking.

The Greek novelist Nikos Kazantzakis (famous for his novel-turned-into-film, *Zorba the Greek)* wrote in a letter to his wife in 1925:

> *"The ultimate, most holy form of theory is action . . . ."*

So when prognosticating is in lieu of action, it may range from worthless to harmful. A strategy is a form of theory or of prognosticating. If the theory or the plan is provisional—that is, subject to infinite revision and improvisation as the consequences emerge—then it is of potential value.

> *It is better to do life well than to theorize about it.*

The English writer Dorothy L. Sayers, famous for her detective stories, once quipped:

> *"Very dangerous things, theories."*

Given that detectives and their adversaries alike depend upon having theories (or hypotheses, or prognostications) about what will happen if one thinks about it this or that way, she is probably saying that a premature or wrong theory gets in the way of a right one. Given that we can't do without them, it's a matter of how they turn out.

But *doing life* as you would have it done depends upon how you perform your life. It does not depend entirely on how you project it. Rather than relying on predictions, if you intend to be one of those doing life as they would have it done you have to develop yourself in the context of the real world.

Don't impose your private theories on the real world. Let the real world impose itself on you. In the ever-changing context of the real world, you need to theorize against the realities you face, not those dictated by some rigid beliefs that travel with you.

Doing life means being open to life. Life is not a theory. You cannot *be* a theory and do life as you would have it done in this irrational social world you actually inhabit.

What you can't actually accomplish in that world is a way of doing life you can't imagine. You are merely the instrument of doing life in that world. Perfect the instrument, not the world.

> *"Prophecy is the most gratuitous form of error."*
> —George Eliot (pseud.), 1872

IX

. . . Problems and Predicaments

"I have yet to see any problem, however
complicated, which when you looked at it in the
right way, did not become still more complicated."

—Paul Alderson, in *New Scientist,* 1969

"Problems are the price of progress: don't
bring me anything but trouble—good news
weakens me . . . ."

—Charles F. Kettering

As long as you are alive, you will have problems. If you can't make enough for yourself, you will have friends and acquaintances who will enthusiastically contribute to your tote bag of problems.

Then there are always the commercial media. They will regularly tell you what problems are in fashion, and then sell you what you need to treat them.

A *problem* is, as you know, an irritating discrepancy between the way things are supposed to be (in your view) and the way things seem to be. It's like having an itch and being compelled to scratch it. Anything that removes the irritation might be acceptable as treatment for the problem.

The humorist Evan Esar offers a comment for fun to launch us into this subject:

"Wouldn't it be wonderful if life's big problems occurred
when we're seventeen—and know everything?"

Yet, as we also know, teenagers seem to have more problems than their elders. Their suicide rate is higher. That solves *their* problems. But it creates a problem for others.

Maybe there's more than meets the eye at first reading of his quip. Such as:

- The problems we face are caused by other people solving *their* problems (or so they think this is all they're doing).

- Even though we were probably complicit in creating them, problems seem to appear uninvited.

- Whether or not a problem is a "big" problem depends upon who has it and how troublesome it is for the one who has it.

- You might think that *knowing everything* would enable a person to escape problems before they occur.

- But the more we know, the more problems we have—and the "bigger" and more complicated they seem to be.

- You might also think that the older we get and the more experience we have, the fewer our problems would be and the easier they would be to handle. Do you know of any older people who would agree with this?

- If you have no particular aim in life, you will have problems. If you have aims in life, you will encounter even more—and more challenging—problems.

- So why would anyone try to do *anything*? Why go out of your way to make problems for yourself? Why not be satisfied with the problems that everyone else has?

There are two kinds of dots we "connect" to string together the story of our lives. One is our past joys or exhilarations. The other is our past problems and difficulties. They are how we punctuate the stories of our lives.

The advantage of having aims in life is that the problems you have are those you have created by the nature of your journey. Otherwise, you are stuck with the common or popular problems of the day.

In that sense, you *choose* the kinds of problems you will have.

There is this old, probably apocryphal, saying:

> *Solutions multiply problems.*

People often ignore the fact that solutions to problems in the "real" world often if not always have consequences in the real world. So "solving" a problem may eliminate *that* problem. But the solution may have consequences that turn out to be worse problems than the one you just solved.

There is no remedy for this. It simply requires that you look at a solution to a problem in terms of the problems that may emerge from the solution you impose.

Bacteria, for example, are adversarial. Put together some medicine to attack and kill bacteria, and they do some shape-shifting, becoming immune to that medication. Then we have a new and more challenging problem than we had at the outset.

Most solutions to problems end up generating other, often more complex, problems. There are no solutions which, in their consequences, do not generate other problems.

Alvin Toffler, famous for his book *Future Shock*, had this to say in another book, *The Third Wave*:

> "All social and political problems are interwoven—that
> energy, for example, affects economics, which in turn
> affects health, which in turn affects education, work,
> family life, and a thousand other things. The attempt to
> deal with neatly defined problems in isolation from one
> another . . . creates only confusion and disaster."

Everything belongs to a *system* of things. And as systems thinkers have long known, you cannot change just one thing in a system because it will impact everything else in that system. You have to change the whole system. If you don't deal with it as a whole, you will create more problems than you imagine you have solved.

An organization, for example, cannot be fixed piecemeal. Every part of the organization is related to every other part. A change in one part can influence the functioning of every other part.

The same is true for individuals, because the individual is a system. Just because physicians specialize these days doesn't mean that solving a problem with your digestive tract may not cause problems somewhere else. If you are a hand specialist the joke is, which finger? Physicians do not treat whole persons. They treat specific problems as if they were unrelated to the whole.

You might be able to take a watch apart to see what its problem is. But that does not guarantee you could put it back together in working order. Analyzing things has its place. But people and their organizations and institutions and their lives are not things.

Physicists have long known that observing the phenomena they observe actually affects how they behave. Their operations have been altered merely by observing them.

Like your body, your life is a complex system. You cannot fix it by altering or adding or subtracting one thing. Any partial change affects everything else.

Doing life is a whole—it is a complex system. And it is interwoven with other lives. You can't fix the problem in isolation. You have to fix the system.

That's why "motivation" doesn't work. It doesn't change anything beyond one's immediate thinking and feeling. That's only a part of the system to which you belong.

Doing life as you would have it done requires systems thinking. Who or what do you belong to? What or who belongs to you? You may not be able to fix your financial problems without fixing at the same time your spiritual problems. You can't simply solve *your* problem. You have to fix the problems of the *context* in which you have—or would like to have—your life.

You have your life in the *experience* of living. Carburetors don't. Your experiences are private and totally **not** interchangeable. You can't have my experience. I can't have your experience.

The experience of life you will have depends upon how you go about *doing life*. You first have to decide how you intend to *experience* life. The activities you engage in are not your life. They are what produce your life—they are means to an end. The consequences of how you perform your life are the cumulative experiences of your life. It is the consequences you are after, not the activities.

The Italian novelist and short-story writer Alberto Moravia made this intriguing observation in *The Time of Desecration* (1967):

> *"In life there are no problems, that is, objective and external choices; there is only the life which we do not resolve as a problem but which we live as an experience, whatever the final result may be."*

A problem is a troublesome variation from what we are accustomed to. What you are most accustomed to is the life you have had up to this point in time. You do not see your life—your accumulated sense of identity—as the problem. You see anything that threatens the life you are used to as a problem.

What threatens the life you are used to may be precisely your wake-up call. But you will likely treat it as something to be ignored or exterminated.

The inertial forces of the life you have had and are living are powerfully resistant to change. They affect the way you perceive things going on around you. We shy away from experiences that might change us in any significant way. We want the experiences of a life that is familiar to us.

We want to stay on the path we're on whatever the final result may be.

We prefer the problems to which we have a ready solution. We prefer the problems that keep us on the trajectory we're on.

The final result may not be what we want. This is a disturbing paradox. You may want to be someone else—better, perhaps. But you will likely shun the very problems that would get you there.

> *Doing life as you would have it done requires you to choose the problems which can make that way of life possible.*

Most people do not change all that much over their lifetimes, once the trajectory of their lives has been firmly established. People may *say* they are not satisfied with the lives they have. They may *say* they would rather be the kind of person they dream of. But they won't do it because it is too scary a task.

Once you become who you *are*, the forces of habit take over. They are stronger than your willpower or your desires, as we have seen. Your life may not be what you want. But you are embedded in a support system that will keep you as you are.

Doing life otherwise requires you to change that whole support system. Even then, there are no guarantees. You have to move from the familiar to the unfamiliar. That inspires fear and hesitation.

Doing life as you would have it done is far, far easier to talk about than to carry out.

There is in addition a short litany of insights into the problem-having/problem-solving process that would serve well anyone who intends to *do* life rather than being done-to *by* life:

- Given the necessity of interpreting everything that occurs to you or happens to you, start with the fact that what you recognize as a problem depends upon the mental models by which you perceive the world.

- If there is something that seems wrong going on, you have to *name* that problem.

- You set about solving the problem that has been named, which may not be the real problem.

- The Western mindset seems to favor fixing symptoms, not the underlying cause of the problem you see and name. If you treat the symptoms, the underlying problem will persist. For example, if the underlying problem in any group effort is incompetence, you may be inclined to treat the symptoms of incompetence, and not the underlying source.

- The well-known broadcaster Eric Sevareid gave voice to a paradox long known when he said,

"The chief cause of problems is solutions."

- What could this mean except that the solutions people believe they have in their toolboxes determine the kinds of problems they see? This is related to the old saying, "If all you have is a hammer, everything looks like a nail." It is the solutions we assume we can bring to bear that largely determine the problems we see and name.

- The difference between achievers and non-achievers is that achievers do a far better job of seeing, naming, and dealing with their problems, at the level of the *source* of those problems.

- If you treat doing life as a problem unique to you, that only you can solve, you will be better off than starting with some faddish set of techniques.

- If you view yourself as the problem, you will do a much better job than if you view the world outside of you as the problem. It is your ability to adapt and move forward that matters. Everything else will be whatever we say it is.

- Competent people do not waste their time on problems they can do nothing about—like the ones that have already occurred, or the ones that others cling to because they are a part of that person's self-image, or the ones they couldn't do anything about even if they wanted to—like "the economy" or the norms of others.

- In a group context, if it doesn't make any difference who gets credit for solving a problem, it will be better named and dealt with.

- Avoid 90% of talk about problems. The solution to any problem is in the action you take.

- Don't just solve problems. *Obviate* them—which means roughly making their reoccurrence impossible.

For some people, a problem is a burden to bear. For others, it is an opportunity—a chance to learn and grow. People who perceive and name the right problems will relish them—as Kettering said at the top of this chapter. Thomas Edison literally created the problems he had to solve in order to achieve his purposes. So did Michelangelo. So did Alexander the Great. So does every jazz improviser. So do those who truly love one another. So does everyone who commits to a purpose in life.

There are no problems in the world outside of you, as Moravia reminded us. *Problems exist only in and for people.* The world is the way it is because it got to be that way. No problem there.

Don't take a stand atop your past solutions of your past problems.

"Dr. Seuss" (Theodor Seuss Geisel) had a wry observation on the universality of problems:

> *"It's a troublesome world. All the people who're in it*
> *Are troubled with troubles almost every minute.*
> *You ought to be thankful, a whole heaping lot,*
> *For the places and people you're lucky you're not."*

The insight here, perhaps, is that you may have problems, but given the sheer number of other people who have problems almost every minute you should be thankful you are not them.

Some people are hoarders. They gather as many problems as they can find, and hoard them. Some people actually make a life out of having problems. It's a strange and irrational thing. But *doing life* means you will make a life out of whatever is available to you—mentally, emotionally, and physically.

It doesn't mean that every attempt you make to do life as you would have it done is inevitably going to improve your circumstances. It merely makes that *possible*. But whether it is a good thing or bad depends upon the richness and the depth of your understanding of those possibilities.

The imperative lesson here is this:

> *The life you **do** can never be any better than who you*
> ***are**—morally, intellectually, emotionally.*
>
> *Doing life as you would have it done depends upon the*
> ***character** you equip yourself to bring to it.*

No life is problem-free. Everything depends upon the qualities (and the competencies) you can muster to deal with what occurs. The thinner your resources, the thinner and more precarious your life will be.

In his own curmudgeonly way, the Austrian philosopher of the language of life Ludwig Wittgenstein once wrote:

> *"The solution of the problem of life is seen in the*
> *vanishing of the problem."*

He was also a virtuoso whistler.

His cryptic comment can be taken in two ways:

- One, the prospect that your problems will be over when you die. They will then vanish.

- The other is that if you make the problem of life vanish by simply *doing* your life, then that's one problem you won't have to deal with.

There was a Japanese psychologist named Shoma Morita who was a contemporary of Freud's but who had a radically different perspective on living life. Freud's psychology is a "deficit" psychology—focusing on what we don't have but may need in our lives. Morita's psychology focuses on how actions taken in the everyday world can eliminate troublesome emotions and so-called mental problems.

For example, if you feel depressed, clean your home thoroughly. Thinking about doing *that* when you are engaged in it will make your feelings of depression fade away into the background.

A physician himself, Dr. Morita believed that:

> *"In fact, it is our effort to change our feelings that often makes us feel even worse,"* and that

> *". . . in actuality, it is not necessary to change our feelings in order to take action."*

This action-oriented kind of psychology is far more conducive to the project of *doing life* than is analysis. The more you analyze (or just talk about your problems), the more inwardly-focused you will be, the more self-centered you will become. You need to be liberated from self-centeredness. You need to be outwardly-focused, on what you are trying to accomplish and not what your problems of the moment may be.

People who have few problems are not those who boldly embrace doing life. In fact, the opposite is true. People who are doing life rather than having life done to them usually have *more* problems than do purposeless people. They do life *in spite of* the problems they face. They do not waste their energies on their problems. They conserve them for their aims in life—for *doing life*.

Doing life begins with doing one's duty. We may see our duty. We may know what it is. But doing life as you would have it done requires fulfilling your duty—to yourself, to others, to your community, and to your society.

The German-born (1749-1832) scientist-poet Johann Wolfgang von Goethe offered this definition of duty:

> *"Duty: where one loves what one orders oneself to do."*

If there are not things that you are duty-bound to do—for yourself for others—you are not doing life. You are merely a passive observer of life.

Goethe's definition suggests that one should love doing what one orders oneself to do. This raises the question of what sort of *conscience* people have. Some people have very strong consciences. They do what they tell themselves to do. Others have very weak consciences—sometimes, judging from their behavior, non-existent.

Doing life requires you to have a powerful and well-trained conscience. Since habits actually energize and direct your behavior, it is your habits that underwrite most of your behavior. But if there are times when you must ponder what you should or should not do, you will discuss this with your conscience—that small voice inside your head.

If you have learned how to behave conscientiously (not the easiest course, as everyone who has ever aspired to be the authors of their own lives learns), you will do your duty. And you will love doing what you order yourself to do.

"Duty" is not a very popular idea these days. But most people prefer to have their lives in the anonymous masses. They think and act and have and do and say what others do, assuming that this is the path to take since others are taking it. For example, people buy the best-sellers, not because this is what they personally need to construct and fuel their own lives, but just so they can be in the know. Talking about what is known by the people you talk to most often is often a substitute for your duty to yourself.

William Penn, who founded what became the state of Pennsylvania and who was persecuted back in England for his Quaker faith, once remarked,

"Do good with what thou hast, or it will do thee no good."

It was his faith (*his* conscience) speaking of course. But he was setting forth the proposition that doing life as it should be done was a matter of doing good with whatever you have and whoever you are. Not only will failing to do so "do thee no good," but it will affect you negatively.

You need to ponder this:

*A life without imperatives for how to do it right is a poor
life indeed. Doing life right means that you will love doing
what you have ordered yourself to do.*

*What matters is not what happens to you. What matters
is what you do with what happens to you.*

*You are the only person on earth who has access to your
inner life. If that is not what it should be, you cannot be who
you would be.*

And, lest we forget, the American novelist and essayist Christopher Morley
left us this to chew on:

*"There are three ingredients in the good life: learning,
earning, and yearning."*

The other two depend upon the first.

Predicaments

A *predicament* is a problem caused by ourselves. They are the most difficult
to treat, because the owner of the predicament has a vested interest in the
continuation of the predicament.

A predicament ensues when you are your own problem. It is most often the
case that people are the source of their own problems. When *you*
are the problem, you have to *solve* yourself.

When the problem persists or recurs—when, that is, it becomes a
predicament—you can know that you are the problem.

- The world you live in is constantly changing.

- The world you live in is indifferent to your personal problems.

- Thus if they persist or recur, you know that it is you—not the world you inhabit—that is the problem.

The famous Swiss psychiatrist Carl Jung, who early on collaborated with Freud and later challenged Freud's dogma, wrote:

> *"The greatest and most important problems of life are insoluble. They can never be solved but only outgrown."*

Doing life as it should be done is the only known way of outgrowing those problems.

X

. . . Causes and Consequences

"The greatest griefs are those we cause ourselves."

—Sophocles (in *Oedipus Rex,* c. 430 B.C.)

"The law of unintended consequences pushes us ceaselessly through the years, permitting no pause for perspective."

—Richard Schickel (in *Time,* 1983)

Our cultural inheritance gives us two ways of looking at the world:

- Looking back, as at history, for what caused what; and

- Looking around at the present, wondering how all this happened.

Every civilization has had similar curiosities. The difference is that our "modern" culture has been infected by the quasi-scientific notion developed in laboratories, of the single cause with single effect. In the pseudo-sciences, this is C—> E—that is, what caused this effect or, alternatively how can we "cause" a specified effect?

In psychology, one of the pseudo-sciences now popularized into folkloristic dogma, it is S—> R: what was the stimulus or the cause for this response? Or, alternatively, if you wanted to bring about a desired response, what would you use as stimulus or cause for that?

Given the "real" world outside our little psyches, this is pretty thin gruel. For two reasons:

One is that a single cause can have many consequences, and that a singular circumstance we may be observing could have had many different "causes."

The other reason that our reductionist orientation is thin if not actually misleading is what has come to be called "the law of unintended consequences." In the real world what we try to cause by some action may not result in what we intended. It may also have consequences that we did *not* intend.

So simplistic notions of cause and effect, or stimulus and response, serve us poorly in the real world, no matter how well they may seem to work in the laboratory.

That kind of thinking causes more problems than it could possible solve. For example, you might profess your love to someone, or try to "motivate" someone in your family or social circle to do this or that for their own good. The consequences of your intended good may turn out to be the opposite of what you intended.

The person in the first case may say "I'm flattered," but still be offended. You can't persuade someone to love you. It doesn't work that way.

In the second case your interest or advice may be unwelcome. When you say or do something, you may be well-intentioned. But it is others who interpret you. They are usually not obligated to substitute your intentions for their interpretations.

You might egoistically buy into the notion that people will interpret what you say or do the way you do. If they did, you would *always* lose at checkers or chess. Or even at love or leadership.

People can't "read" your mind. You can't "read" their minds. As a practical matter you should, if you want to do life well, *never* even try to do so. The best relationships are always those in which there are ultimately unknowns.

Now the question arises: how will you "cause" yourself in the right way if the consequences are not certain? Pop psychology makes it all sound so simple. If you just do this or that, the results will be what you desire. Those who peddle easy short-cuts to the good life are our present-day snake-oil purveyors. They have no investment in you beyond the point of sale.

> *There is nothing that is simple or easy about doing life the way you would have it done. If there were, we'd all be saints. Advice is cheap. Doing a truly worthy life is not. It has a price to be paid.*

Ralph Waldo Emerson once wrote:

> *"A foolish consistency is the hobgoblin of little minds . . . ."*
> *Is it so bad, then, to be misunderstood? Pythagoras was*
> *misunderstood, and Socrates, and Jesus, and Luther,*
> *and Copernicus, and Galileo, and Newton, and every*
> *pure and wise spirit that ever took flesh. To make a*
> *difference is to be misunderstood.*

Pragmatically, what he is suggesting is that if you are learning, if you are growing, if you are trying to become something better or more than you are, you will appear to others to be inconsistent. So be it. They prefer that you do not change so they don't have to change. They would keep you as you are.

Your life—or mine—has to look like small potatoes compared to those illustrious figures who changed history. But that is not Emerson's point. His point is that anyone's life is a history of that person. To change the course of that person's history would be an equivalent achievement. And there is only one person who can achieve that—you.

Better that others may misunderstand you than that you should misunderstand yourself. And if you take their word for who you are and who you ought to be, you are misunderstanding yourself.

To change the course of your life is just as "great" as what those people did. They just happened to end up on a larger stage. But that's an historical artifact. They didn't set out to be the persons historians made them out to be. They were simply *doing life*—the kind of life they chose. That they were misunderstood was not something *they* caused.

The misunderstanding was caused by the way *others* interpreted *them*. If you do your life the way you should, you may not change the history of the world. But you will change your own history. And that is just as difficult and just as laudatory an achievement.

Consider carefully the observation made by Richard Schickel at the top of this chapter. He wrote,

> *"The law of unintended consequences pushes us ceaselessly through the years, permitting no pause for perspective."*

You may have assumed that he meant something about the sweep of history (again on the big stage). But it could also be taken as an observation on individual lives. You get "pushed ceaselessly" through *your* years, giving you nothing permanent to stand on for perspective.

We live our lives in the flurry of the days. We have raised our happengs to an avocation. The small world in which we live our lives is changing more rapidly—even fluidly. There are those all-important *UNINTENDED CONSEQUENCES* from what we did or did not do yesterday. And there are those unintended consequences from what others did or did not do yesterday and all the days before that.

We may say to others whom we have afflicted: "I didn't mean to do that." But a deed once done cannot be retracted. We are asking forgiveness when we should have asked for permission to do harm.

Or we may say to others: "I didn't *mean* it that way!" But something once said and interpreted cannot be reversed. We can never go back to the way things were. There is only today and tomorrow.

Intended consequences are one thing. But unintended consequences are an entirely different thing. We don't live in a world of intentions. We live in a world of things said or done—as they are interpreted by others.

Doing life well depends on the **consequences** *of your behavior and your words. Life cannot be lived in your intentions. To be the cause of your life means being the cause of your life in the real world—not in your ruminations about it.*

When we look back on our lives, we are different people than we were when those thoughts and actions (the personal "causes") actually took place. A perspective is always a *present* perspective. We rarely see ourselves as we *are*. We see ourselves as we *were*, or as we might wish to be. We forgive ourselves our trespasses. Others often will not.

You can only understand yourself looking back or looking forward. The present is the only place there is for you to make good on your intentions. You can't change the past. You can't predict the future. Doing life as you would have it done requires you to assume responsibility for who you were in the past, and thus for who you will become in the future, using the raw material you have in the present.

Lyndon B. Johnson (the 36th President of the U.S.) often spoke epigrammatically. Useful to us here is a comment he made in September 1967:

> *"There are plenty of recommendations on how to get out of trouble cheaply and fast. Most of them come down to this: Deny your responsibility."*

We already know that there is a surfeit of advice on how to treat your present troubles and problems—both cheap and fast. But that kind of advice comes with an enormous price tag. The price is that of denying your responsibility.

People are easily addicted to that. But that creates an even more insoluble problem. If you are not responsible for your past actions, then you will imperceptibly lose sight of the possibility for being responsible for how you do life today and tomorrow. Denying responsibility takes away your potential for doing life as you would have it done.

If you do not assume responsibility for your past, and if you deny responsibility for who you are today in the midst of what is gong on today, there is little to no possibility for you to take over the reins of your own life.

You can't do life as you would have it done if you are habituated to being done-to *by* life.

The logic here is tenacious and implacable. The unintended consequence of denying responsibility for yourself is that you lose the leverage required for doing life as you would have it done.

> *You can't be a doer of life if you are an accomplished*
> *victim of circumstances. You can't be the **cause** of who*
> *you become if you are satisfied to be the **consequence**.*

The British novelist and influential critic Arnold Bennett once remarked:

> *"You are not in charge of the universe; you are in*
> *charge of yourself."*

It seems that most people despair of ever being in charge of themselves, and so busy themselves with trying to be in charge of the universe—i.e., the other people they know, the organizations they belong to, and the political scene in general. That's akin to the old saying, "The grass is always greener on the other side of the fence."

Other people's problems seem simpler and more fixable than one's own, so what are they wringing their hands about?

The changes other people would have to make seem less drastic than our own, so why are they reluctant to do what needs doing?

People who don't complain about their problems must have less onerous problems—so we can feel superior to them.

What gets forgotten in this rush to solve other people's problems (or gigantic socio-political problems) is that our own lives are a consequence of how we *cause* ourselves. The consequences which constitute the part of your life that you *can* control are inherent is the causes that you initiated in all of your yesterdays.

We might imagine that we are merely doing what needs to be done on a daily basis. But how you think about things, and how you do things, has both consequences for you and for all of the other people and conditions that fill your life.

If you enable things, you necessarily also constrain things. That's the way systems work. What you do or don't do today creates the possibilities and the limitations of what you can or can't do in the future. In the same way, what you did or did not do in the past creates the possibilities and the limitations of what you can do—or be—in the present and the future.

Life is a continuum. You can't go back and change anything. You can't go forward except as you are built to do so. You have to make your life out of the qualities you have to make it with. No one else can do this for you. Nothing you possess can do this for you.

As it is written in the ancient Hindu Upanishads,

> "What one does and what he thinks, that he becomes."

We may not be fully responsible for the kind of person we ultimately become. But as this suggests, we can be and are *responsible* for what we do and how we think. That's where *doing life* begins—at the level of what you do and what you think. In this sense, you are both the cause and the consequence of your life.

Stanislaw Lec presented us with a very provocative metaphor. He wrote (in his *More Unkempt Thoughts, 1968):*

> "No snowflake in an avalanche ever feels responsible."

The most obvious interpretation is that being an anonymous part of a crowd of anonymous people removes the burden of your own personal responsibility for what you do or how you think. And that's the kind of world we live in. We are in large numbers like an avalanche on our way to an unknown, uncertain future.

We pell-mell try to keep up with the latest fashions, not only in clothing, homes, and cars, but in what we think, what we believe, what we say, and what we do. Along with the comfort of the crowd, our culture actually encourages us to be the victims of this crowd culture. Our policies are more about saving the victims than about rewarding those who might lead us in better ways. That might even be you.

Of course you are not a "snowflake." But whatever is faddish will draw something like an avalanche down upon it. Even the "best-sellers" work that way. If a new idea or a new electronic toy comes along and gains traction, people flock to it like snowflakes to an avalanche—thoughtlessly.

IF you would do life as you would have it done, you have to choose:

- Either you will end up being one of the *unintended* consequences, being done-to by the maelstrom of social and intellectual and emotional forces swirling around you 24/7; or

- To become optimally the *intended* consequence of the kind of life you ought to have for your own benefit and that of your society.

The kind of *laissez-faire* culture we inhabit today will not do this for you. It is indifferent to what you become. It has its interests only in what you do to increase the crowd appeal of whatever is fashionable day to day. Your culture doesn't care about you personally. Nor does it care about your destiny in this world of ours. It "cares" only about furthering the causes of which it is already the unintended consequences.

If you are certain that is the right direction, then tumble on in the avalanche. If you are not certain, you have some work to do.

Procrastination thus has its upside. If you lag behind the social and ideological magnets of the day, you may escape them. Tomorrow they will be different. If you put off joining the "avalanches" long enough, they may come around again.

But there is one thing about which no one of us can afford to procrastinate. We rarely know what the effects of our procrastinations may be. Sometime we get lucky. Yet here is a situation where the effects of procrastination are certain.

IF you intend to do life as you would have it done, you have to get started today. Because each day you fail to do so, the trajectory of the life you presently have is further locked into place. With each passing day you don't take charge of being the prime mover in your life, old habits and the status quo become more influential.

Ultimately, you won't be able to muster the energy or the desire to do so. What is certain is that if you do not take charge today, the life you presently lead will be one day more embedded and difficult to change.

"We are always getting ready to live, but never living."

That's an observation from one of the best of the philosophers of *doing life*—Emerson. You may "intend" to do so. But we all know what the road to hell is paved with.

You have to learn how to do life by doing it—as Aristotle said. If you want to be a painter, you have to paint. If you want to be a writer, you have to write. Then you learn how to detect your mistakes and your shortfalls, and go at it again. It is the same for learning how to be a stonemason or a parent or a CEO. You undertake it not because you know how to do it. You undertake it because you are committed to learning how to do it better—every day.

If you don't do your life that way, it will never be as you would have it.

"Truth" OR Consequences

It is far more important to do life well than to know the "truth" about doing life well. There is no way of *doing life* other than by doing life.

In our culture, we are obsessed with our pursuit of "the truth" about everything. This has brought us distinct advantages in technology and medicine. But doing life is not about the truth. It is about the conditions of your life.

The problem with the blind pursuit of the truth is that the truth changes when it is decided by the gurus and the guardians of "the truth" that a better truth has come along. And since we are dedicated to the endless pursuit (rather than arriving once and for all), every truth will sooner or later be an untruth.

As a culture, we prefer sleuthing a cause rather than tracking a consequence. We have far more interest in sick people than we do in healthy people. We want fixes for our social and economic problems. But we are indifferent to the consequences—and unintended consequences—of those fixes. Spouses have been know to argue endlessly about who said what. But they do not have the same passion about the consequences of those arguments.

Native American Indians were generally *truth-keepers*. They had long since (for millennia) known what those truths were. The purpose of the elders was to keep those truths alive. Newcomers were taught those truths and were expected to live them. They believed that the ultimate aim in life was beauty, not truth. They already knew what that was.

And they had few if any communicable diseases before the Europeans began to overrun them. They were not obese. Their leaders had to give up all their worldly possessions in order to become the chief. They did not want chiefs who had the power to aggrandize themselves in that role.

There were these and many other advantages. They did not have television or cell phones or the internet. They had no need. It is the widespread adoption of those devices that actually *causes* the need.

They believed not in research nor in theories but in wisdom.

The 20th-century journalist and writer Norman Cousins wrote in *Saturday Review* (in 1978):

> *"Wisdom consists of the anticipation of consequences."*

Wisdom is not to be found in the knowledge we claim about "the truth." It inheres in how a person (or a nation) anticipates the consequences of what is believed or what is done.

In our culture, we are far more into facts than in their consequences.

Doing life as you would have it done requires the growth of wisdom. It requires you to consider the consequences of what you believe or what you do (or what you don't believe and don't do).

To become wise means that you do not tell other people they are wrong. You ask questions. People who are wise do not pontificate. They are curious.

They are first and foremost curious about themselves. How do I "know" that? Why do I believe that? Why would I choose to do that and not something more efficacious?

The inscription above the Oracle at Delphi was the famous, KNOW THYSELF. Wisdom starts with being skeptical of what you know, what you feel, and not how you casually justify your own behavior while criticizing others.

Doing life as you would have it done requires you to examine critically how you came to see life as you do. It requires you to challenge whatever you take for granted. It requires you not always to be right, but to do life in a way that considers first the consequences—for you and for others who may be affected by what you say or what you do.

It requires you to "de-center" yourself—to look at things from others' perspectives and not impose your own perspectives before doing so.

It is knowing what you believe and why. But it is also extending the same prerogative to others. After all, you could both be wrong.

You arrive at the best way of doing life only by the commitment to becoming wiser tomorrow than you were today.

The French essayist and courtier Michel de Montaigne wrote (in his *Essais*—which was a major contribution to literary history, 1572-1580):

"We can be knowledgeable with other men's knowledge,
but we cannot be wise with other men's wisdom."

Wisdom has to be earned by oneself, for oneself. There are no recipes, no secrets, no ten steps to wisdom.

As the journalist and quipster Evan Esar wrote:

"You can only become wise by noticing what happens to
you when you aren't."

And if you can't figure that out, there is little hope for doing life as you would have it done.

Doing life wisely can only be achieved by noticing what happens to you when you don't. You are the cause of those consequences.

[Certain of these major themes will be dealt with in more depth in the chapters ahead. This is not for the purpose of simply repeating them. It is for the purpose of making sure that you have another opportunity to take full note of them—and thus of giving them their due in terms of how critical they are to your full understanding.]

XI

...Frustration and Gratification

"The mass of men lead lives of quiet desperation."

—Henry David Thoreau (1854)

"We will not think noble thoughts because we are not noble. We will not live in beautiful harmony because there is no such thing in this world, nor should there be. We promise only to do our best and live out our lives. Dear God, that's all we can promise in truth."

—Lillian Hellman (1956)

We live in two worlds in our conscious and semi-conscious lives. There is our *inner* world of images, ideas, and scenarios of which we are the sole authors. There is simultaneously the *outer* world of people and *their* perceptions, beliefs, and actions, and of our mutual collectives.

How this world sees us bears upon how we see ourselves. How we see ourselves may not bear heavily on how that world of other people sees us. But how we see ourselves bears heavily upon our inner world and thus upon how we evolve over the years.

There is more or less *frustration* when the life you actually live is inconsistent with your daydreams and schemes about it. There is more or less *gratification* when your inner world and the outer world seem to be in sync. That may not be often. But some people would call it "happiness."

Competence and Happiness

Some people would also believe that the aim in life is to be "happy." But it has long been known that *the direct pursuit of happiness is the surest way of not achieving it.*

As we use the term today, it is more of a talisman than a condition of life. We expose ourselves to thousands of short (as in commercial advertising) to long stories (as on television and in the movies) where the suspense gets resolved by some sort of "happiness." The best example is probably the ending of the many kinds of fairy tales we consume where the people involved "lived happily ever after." It's difficult to know what that might mean in a practical sense. That part of the story—which comes after the ending—is the part that is never revealed to us. "Happily"? How did they do that? And why is how they did that not revealed to us?

"Happiness" may be the modern version of the search for the "Holy Grail." There may not be such a thing. And if there is, what would it take to be able to handle it?

The Irish playwright and social critic George Bernard Shaw (in *Man and Superman*) offered us the extreme view:

> *"A lifetime of happiness! No man alive could bear it: it would be hell on earth."*

That kind of life—being "happy" all the time—would for Shaw be reserved only for idiots. He sees it as a condition of life that would be intolerable because you can't be happy and in touch with the real world at the same time. To be happy means you are living in some sort of dream-world. There are far better aims in any life worth living.

In *The Heart of the Matter,* the prolific English writer Graham Greene identified the source of many of our modern "relationship" problems. As he said,

> *"No human being can really understand another; and no one can arrange another's happiness."*

It often happens that people fall in love because the other person *makes* them happy. Then they fall out of love when the other person no longer *makes* them happy. A relationship based upon what the other person contributes to your happiness is doomed from the outset. Not just because it actually can't be done, but because that is a form of bondage. If you hold the other person even slightly responsible for your happiness, you are also engaging in a form of blackmail—not the best conditions for a healthy relationship.

People have different afflictions, and differing susceptibilities to those afflictions. Happiness may be something like that—some people have it and some people don't. Why?

The so-called English "Gloomy Dean" W. R. Inge once wrote:

> *"The happiest people seem to be those who have no*
> *particular reason for being happy except that they are."*

"Happiness" is ineffable. There may be no reason for being happy except that some people are and some people aren't. Happy people are not necessarily the ones who are doing life as they would have it. Their happiness gets in the way. Unhappy people do life according to how they are able to do so. But their unhappiness gets in the way.

Abraham Lincoln echoed this when he said,

> *"Most folks are about as happy as they make up their*
> *minds to be."*

Is happiness a choice? If so, is unhappiness a choice? In the perspective of doing life as we are developing it here, the answer must surely be "Yes." Maybe that is not a direct choice—but more like a result of cumulative choices over many years. We end up becoming where our choices and our habits lead us. So perhaps it is useful to think of "happiness" not as a goal in life, but as a set of habits built up over time.

On a lighter note, this quip from the humor columnist Evan Esar can make its contribution to our thinking about this:

> *"If ignorance is bliss, why isn't the world happier?"*

He does have a point. If ignorance is bliss, why aren't the people around you happier? Is this what you owe *them*? Are they here to make you happy?

We're exploring the connection between *frustration* and *gratification* here, using "gratification" as a more accurate descriptor of a better way of doing life than happiness. Maybe a satisfying or a gratifying life would be a better descriptor than a "happy" life.

We should know by now that we can't take happiness as a goal. So what is the best way of looking at the role of *competence* in all this?

An observation in his book *Self-Renewal* by John W. Gardner, past President of the Carnegie Foundation and Founder of "Common Cause" may help us get there:

> *"Storybook happiness involves every form of pleasant thumb-twiddling: true happiness involves the full use of one's powers and talents."*

It is more than "full use of one's powers and talents." It is primarily a matter of being fully competent in one's role(s) in the real world. Being good does not make one relevant. But being relevant to society in some positive way makes one good. And it is the gratification that goes with performing one's role(s) *competently* in society that produces what most people would take to be "happiness."

Incompetent people may have their escapist fun. But when they are having fun, they are usually not doing something of relevance to the society. There is no way they could be truly happy. That can occur only in the real world, and only in terms of the relevance of their performance to the best interests of the society.

To be *free* of one's duty to oneself and the larger whole is taken by some as a form of happiness. But that's the sort of happiness George Bernard Shaw spoke of (above)—the delusion that leads to hell on earth.

Happiness is not to be found in an escape from duty, but in the performance of one's duty in an exemplary way.

Performing one's duty (or one's role) in an exemplary way requires a level of competence much under-appreciated in our culture.

We try all kinds of psychological tricks in lieu of this kind of competence. Some people even believe that love or loyalty supersedes competence. The frustration that often arises in marriage is not a failure of love or of loyalty. It is a shortfall in competence.

Even in the faulty way we toss the term happiness around, it never ceases to be a byproduct of competence. If those who are extremely competent at what they do appear to us to be happier than most people, it is because they are more competent—and thus more relevant—than most people.

Whether in making a great marriage or in running a corporation or attending a patient or driving a car, people who are less than competent in their role(s) are dissatisfied, frustrated people deep down. They may not know what the problem is. They may blame anything and everything other than themselves. They are bitter and often disappointed in life.

They don't know why. You do. It is because they are less than competent at performing their roles in society. Because they are less than competent, they are less relevant than those who are competent. And if they are less relevant to the society in which they live, they are less likely to have the kinds of feelings that make them as individuals truly happy.

Let us consider what the same John Gardner wrote in *Saturday Evening Post*, 1 December 1962:

> *"The society which scorns excellence in plumbing because plumbing in a humble activity, and tolerates shoddiness in philosophy because philosophy is an exalted activity, will have neither good plumbing nor good philosophy. Neither its pipes nor its theories will hold water."*

He is pointing toward the source of much of the spreading epidemic of frustration in our society. The source of that epidemic is incompetence. For a variety of reasons, people are less competent than they used to be.

Some scholars who have studied this peculiar phenomenon have argued that we are not as smart as we were 10,000 years ago. That's in part because there was far less to be smart *about* 10,000 years ago. And there were far fewer roles which they had to learn. People lived in tribes and never encountered globalization. They didn't have to talk much because there wasn't much to talk about. People apprised things directly. Their "theories" were mainly about what all could see—the natural world around them.

Like Native American Indians, they performed their few roles expertly. About this they had no choice. Individualism hadn't been invented. There was no *diversity*.

Still, when we wax nostalgically about this kind of simple and leisurely life, we have some justification. People didn't *frustrate* one another by their incompetence. They could be members of that tribe or group only because they performed their role(s) competently.

Gardner's point is that we can be citizens of this great democracy with no particular competencies for being members other than the fact that we were born into it. And we have our "rights"—to do as we please and to hell with the consequences.

The implication is that this is a stupid way to develop a country (or an organization). Increasing numbers of our voters are functionally illiterate. When you call Customer Service, you *expect* to be dealt with incompetently. Inventing a computer program to deal with you hasn't helped much.

If you are immersed in incompetence in the world you inhabit, you are going to be frustrated. If you are frustrated, there is not much incentive for you to be "happy." You can't be satisfied with most of your social and commercial interactions.

So there is reason to believe that a society of incompetents will increase our problems and our physical and mental illnesses. Those are indispensable to what we would like to think of as happiness.

Those who are less than competent cannot be happy with themselves. Those they interact with cannot be happy with them. It's a losing proposition. The only way out is to make people more competent, beginning with parents and children. Competent parents are far more likely to make competent offspring.

Until there is a reversal in the general decline of competence in our society, we can expect more frustration and less real gratification.

It is said that

Misery loves company.

Those who can't (or *won't*) be competent apparently will not be happy until they have made all the rest of us as unhappy as they are.

- It is well to know: Those who would do life as they would have it are up against a larger culture that opposes them and their attempts. There are two things that you need to do:

- Take upon yourself no frustrations that are not self-imposed. You have to get along in the outer world. But you do not have to let it affect you negatively.

Do not expect the outer world to be the source of your gratifications (or your "happiness"). Pick your roles carefully. Provide your gratification for yourself by increasing your competence in all of your own roles daily.

It has been reported that 80% of American households do not buy a book in a year. If this is so, it is easy to see why we are becoming a media ("entertainment") culture.

Gratifications in life come from accomplishments that require ever more competence. The core competence is always your capacity for *thinking*—deeply and broadly. You cannot develop this capacity out of gossip, news, and entertainment. The only way you can develop your own mind is to hone it on the best minds that have ever existed. This requires reading. This requires reading widely and well the best that humankind has thought in the past.

Reading what great minds have pondered opens doors to worlds that would otherwise be closed to you.

People who are companions of the best that has been thought and said seem to have a grasp of the world—and themselves in it—that is denied to those who do not or can not read.

If you are surrounded by the best and the best-informed minds that have ever existed, you can gain this mental horsepower through conversation. But to the extent that your circle of communicants is not of that level, the only recourse you have is through reading what our best thinkers have to say about the things that matter.

Read not to appear learned, or to spice your conversation. Read to learn, to enrich your thinking, to grow your mind and thus your being.

Joseph Addison and Richard Steele, in their 18th-century English essay series entitled *The Tatler*, wrote:

> *"Reading is to the mind what exercise is to the body."*

Good health (a condition of happiness?) requires both. What is not exercised atrophies. Minds die a slow and debilitating death if deprived of exercise—as we have seen increasingly in our own time. Can there be such a correlation between reading and good mental health?

But, again, there is "reading" and then there is *reading*. We have previously acclaimed Ralph Waldo Emerson as a guide for people who want to do life and to do life well. In an address at Harvard University in 1837, he said:

> *"One must be an inventor to read well . . . There is then creative reading as well as creative writing."*

To read well—especially the best writing available—requires a kind of co-authorship. The writer authors the text, and the good reader provides his or her own authorship in how they read, understand, interpret, and implement what they read by how their minds were affected by the reading.

It won't do to read something—even if it is the best. You have to think about it. You have to re-invent it in your own thinking. This is the only way you can *own* what you read.

Doing life well requires you to bring in as advisors the best thinkers and writers you can make available. Doing life well requires you to confront the world with the same range of aggressive mindsets with which it confronts you. Once you lose your capacity for learning, you accuse the world for your frustrations.

This minimizes those frustrations in life because you can outwit them. This optimizes your satisfactions with life (your comfort and good feelings) because you are a more competent and more agile participant.

Those who suffer the most frustrations in life are generally those who do not *see* their complicity in their plight. They therefore assume that if someone would just "fix" those parts of their environment that frustrates them, their problems would be over.

They much prefer to associate with other people who are of the same frame of mind as they are. They agree that their problems are not their fault, but the fault of the society. So they vote for or demonstrate for the kinds of government policies that might ameliorate their frustrations.

At the extreme, these are people who are neither interested in nor equipped to be doing life. They prefer to have life done for them—either by their friends and acquaintances, by God, or by some politician.

They have no concern for the real *causes* of their frustrations. They believe that ameliorating the *symptoms* is the best way of solving their problems.

Much government policy is therefore about treating the symptoms of some group's dissatisfactions. It emerges as a matter of "rights" or of "fairness." Both can be good things. But when they are placed in the service of ameliorating the symptoms of problems in which the constituents are complicit, no real solution is any longer possible.

Things evolve in the direction they are evolving. Is that the right direction for enhancing the kind of lives that best humanize us? This question gets lost in the rush to aid the victims of their symptoms—in spite of whatever their own complicity might have been.

For those who would do life well, it comes down to this:

*If you want to know what kind of life you deserve, look
at the one you've got.*

This is not a matter of being hardhearted or unsympathetic. It is a matter of extracting oneself from the hollow rhetoric and getting down to cases. If you believe you "deserve" a better life than the one you imagine you've got, do something about it.

There is only one person who can have the life you have. That's you. There is one person who has let it get that way. That's you. There is only one person who can "fix" it at the level of its cause. That's you. If you believe you deserve a better life, make it so.

When you involve other people, the cause gets obscured. Only the symptoms can be dealt with. And that does not eliminate the problem. As long as the cause remains, the problem will resurface.

When we choose up sides, what is justice for some will be injustice for others. There is no social fix for personal frustrations that will not create dissatisfactions for others.

There *are* wrongs. There *are* injustices. These are the consequences of how earlier problems were solved. New fixes atop old fixes do not attack the real causes. They merely create more problems.

The famous Norwegian playwright Henrik Ibsen raised a useful question in his play *Ghosts* (1881):

*"To crave for happiness in this world is simply to be
possessed . . . What right have we to happiness?"*

Given the endless sea of problems we have created for ourselves and for others, what right indeed? It may have been our right to provide ourselves (and others) with a world in which to be "happy." But we seem not to know how to do that. The best we can do, as Lillian Hellman says at the top of this chapter, is to do the best we can with the mess we've made. Do we all have an equal right to *that*?

Sympathy and Envy

We could probably all agree that sympathy is a good thing. But maybe we're not looking carefully enough.

If we have sympathy for ourselves given the wrongs committed against us by others, by God, or by biology, we prolong and exacerbate our condition. Does that contribute to our pleasures in life?

The humorist Evan Esar wrote in his column:

> *"To feel sorry for yourself is to waste sympathy on someone who doesn't deserve it."*

But maybe you do. You prolong your frustrations or your personal miseries by ruminating on them at great length. For that kind of complicity in your problems, you may well deserve feeling sorry for yourself. You *are* the one who most deserves it.

Similarly, if we have sympathy for others, we reinforce and prolong their miseries. In what way is this helpful?

For the wit and quipster Oscar Wilde, there is a distinctly different way of thinking about this:

> *"If there was less sympathy in the world, there would be less trouble in the world."*

If troubles are perverse, then sympathy for those who have troubles is even more perverse. Here's the thought model behind this: Our troubles expand to accommodate the well of sympathy ready to be lavished upon them.

After all, our physical problems seem to increase exponentially at the same rate as the palliatives for them. Why wouldn't the same be true for our feelings?

Even though the correlations are clearly there, this may not be the case. But it does remain the case that the more we dwell upon our own or others' illnesses or infirmities, the more we keep their miseries alive and even growing.

The illusions we have about "happiness" may be a bit like that. That richest kind of happiness may visit us as a surprise. We forget that it is not something we have, but something that has us. It comes on its own time, and leaves in the same way.

The pianist and humorist Oscar Levant purportedly said on his deathbed:

> *"Happiness isn't something you experience; it's something you remember."*

Or something you yearn for in the future. It is either something we hope for or something we remember. In both cases, it is born of our imagination and plays all of its games there.

In his Foreword to his 1964 play *After the Fall*, Arthur Miller wrote as follows:

> *"Where choice begins, paradise ends, innocence ends, for what is Paradise but the absence of any need to choose this action?"*

So if happiness is a condition akin to paradise, it follows that choosing it is a condition antithetical to achieving it. Here it blooms its full paradoxical nature.

To *sympathize* with a person or a people because they are in misery and are not happy is to choose what can't be chosen. We merely enhance their pain by talking about it in public, making it thereby more real. This is surely a primary example of the law of unintended consequences. As Abraham Heschel said, what is required is not sympathy, but action.

So we are left with the unintended consequences of the opposite of sympathy—*envy*.

They are worth considering. If you are seized by envy, that elevates the status of the person or persons you envy. At the same time, it lowers your status.

That answers the question, what does envy have to do with doing life? Simple, don't do it. Never be envious. It may help the other person, indirectly. But it harms you. Become increasingly competent every day and accomplish what you need to accomplish. Then you can be envious of yourself. Just don't let anyone see this. They will interpret it as arrogance.

Our favorite satirist Evan Esar quipped:

> *"If envy were a disease, everyone would be sick."*

Everyone but you, perhaps. When you have an aim in life, you have no reason to be envious. There will always be those who are more fortunate than you. There will always be others who are less fortunate then you. Go after what you want in doing life. But don't envy the person who has more than you have. It may not be their fault.

Similarly, don't waste your sympathy on those less fortunate. They may have more provided by themselves than they need. If you put them down with your sympathy, you both lose.

Francis Bacon said, *"Envy has no holidays."* Put yours on permanent holiday.

Theodore Roosevelt observed in 1900:

> *"The vice of envy is . . . always a confession of inferiority."*

Keep your confessions private. If, as he suggests, envy is a vice, do not commit it. That status and hierarchy both play a role in life, you must earn your place on your own terms. They are the only terms that are not fickle.

The 17th-century philosopher Baruch Spinoza wrote:

> *"To an envious man nothing is more delightful than another's misfortune, and nothing more painful than another's success."*

Doing life well requires you to take just the opposite stance: delight in others' successes, pained (but discretely so) by their misfortunes. Your life will be better, and thus theirs. This may be hard to do. But it is indispensable to your peace of mind.

You will avoid frustrations and achieve personal satisfactions at the same time.

Pride is another slippery slope. It may seem old-fashioned in the current cultural environment. But anyone who is serious about doing life well should probably revisit a modern version of the "Seven Deadly Sins."

As the 17th-century essayist La Rochefoucauld set forth in his *Maxims*:

> *"Nature . . . endowed us with pride to spare us the pain*
> *of knowing our imperfections."*

His point is the very pragmatic one that a surfeit of pride makes it impossible to see our own imperfections—or to hear about them from others.

Doing life well is not a matter of perfecting yourself. It is more a matter of avoiding the self-protective armor that keeps you from seeing yourself as you truly are. You have to start there. Most people start from the wrong place, and thus usually arrive at a place they never intended.

There is always a paradox that lies in wait for the prideful person. It is easy enough to please yourself, and to gather around you people who will help you be pleased with yourself even if that takes you in the wrong direction.

If you learn how to do life well, you should be proud of yourself. Just make sure that the reasons for being proud of yourself are the right ones.

The critic and "new intellectual" of the 20th-century, Susan Sontag, wrote in her *Death Kit*:

> *"He who despises himself esteems himself as a*
> *self-despiser."*

What we see in the mirror is not what others see. Turning a frustration into a virtue is not the way to go. Happiness may be self-delusion. It won't get you where you want to go.

"It isn't the things a man can do that he is proudest of. It's the things he thinks he can do."

—Evan Esar

XII

. . . Who You Are and Who You Aren't

"If we weren't all so interested in ourselves, life would be so uninteresting we couldn't endure it."

—Arthur Schopenhauer

"It is as hard to see oneself as to look backward without turning around."

—Henry David Thoreau

The "self" is a troublesome concept. It is central to pop psychology and to the self-help industry.

It is central to our culture. The belief there is that we have a "self" that is a more or less fixed entity, but is yet subject to remodeling by our own volition. Implicit in this mythology is that the "self" is substantive and is something we *have*. It is something that belongs to us. It is the core of who we "are."

It is something to be nurtured. It is something to be protected against all outside attempts to change it or malign it. We're addicted to the pop psych attractions of the "self." It's a hazardous addiction. It is also fundamentally wrong-headed.

The influential French writer and bon vivant Andre Gide may be said to be the father of the self-help industry when he wrote:

"Dare to be yourself."

For those who are propelled and equipped to make a substantive contribution to the world of art or of music, this may be a useful aphorism. But for those who have neither the purpose nor the talent to change the world by their creative offerings, it is merely inspirational. It offers hope that will be dashed.

To "dare" to step outside the norms of one's culture is indeed risky. And if the fruits it bears turn out to be worthless, doing so may bear a better risk analysis. Gide could do so. He inherited the wealth that afforded him a platform and a safety net from which to contemplate his "self." If you have these and want to indulge yourself, you may do yourself little harm. But ideas have consequences. And the consequences of this idea can be poisonous to a society. They are to our society.

Here's why.

The Source of "Self"

No human is born with a "self." It is something that has to be partially imposed by others, partly authored beyond that by oneself, IF others endorse your auditions. At most, we may be born with the proclivity for self-reflection. But we cannot be self-reflective (self-aware) until we have some language for doing so.

You can't be aware of being a self amongst other selves until you can talk to them and yourself about it. That capacity you do not have at birth.

In a letter to a friend in 1775, the famous German thinker, poet, and philosopher Johann Wolfgang von Goethe wrote:

> *"One does not get to know that one exists until one [discovers] oneself in others."*

It is how others define us that provides our first definition of ourselves. It is how others see us and define us that provides us with the external parameters of our lives from then on. We may improvise within those limits. But if we overstep them, others will either question us or warn us.

We have the selves that others make possible. We have the selves that we can imagine for ourselves, as long as others endorse our performance of those imagined selves.

Where this leads us is that we become in large part how others define us. What matters most is *who those others are*, and how they define us. It is their world in which we must live outwardly.

This is what the philosopher Cioran meant when he said that

> *"The most important decision you make in your life is who to have as parents."*

Our parents and their circle provide the earliest foundations of who we "are." After awhile it is our peers who establish the possibilities and the constraints on who we become. The other stories and ideas we consume may influence us one way or the other. The choices we make and the performances we turn in as persons in other people's purview affect us.

You may choose to "be" this or that. But it may be possible—or not possible—depending upon who you are and upon the people you hang out with. When you mess with the image they have of you, you are messing with their own identities. You are free only within such limits.

You have to be constantly auditioning for the way you want to be defined by others. If you are successful, they will cast you in the role you want. If your audition is not successful, you remain as they defined you previously.

Who you have already become is the 800-pound gorilla. Who you "are" at any given moment is the largest determiner of who you will become. Technically, this is referred to as *entelechy*—that things (including you) are always in the process of becoming what is possible, and what is most likely.

The inertial forces at work in your life will always be formidable obstacles to any choices you might want to make.

That same Andre Gide (as above) wrote in his journal in 1916:

"Everything in me calls out to be revised, amended, reeducated."

You may as well be moderately dissatisfied with who you "are." You would like to change your circumstances. You must first realize that you can do so only by changing your definition of yourself. This is as scary as it is difficult.

It means your friends can't continue on as your friends. You may need different auditors. It means the way of life you are familiar with has got to be destroyed. It means you have to be better at auditioning for your new role(s) than you presently are. It means you could fail.

One "Self" . . . or Many?

The American psychologist who argued articulately for pragmatism in our understanding of ourselves and the world around us—William James—also said that we do not have "a" self but many selves.

What he meant was that in the course of your life you play many roles. You are a different person with others when you are in a different role. The CEO of a large corporation is not the "boss" of everyone at home or when with his or her peers. A mother to her children cannot be the mother of everyone she meets. A spouse is not the same person with a lover as he or she is at home.

We may be confident in the ruts of our well-used roles. But, as Woody Allen once remarked,

"Confidence is what you have before you understand the problem."

A person is not the same person when becoming a failure as he was when becoming a success. We can have "confidence" only when those around us are playing the roles we expect of them. A fearsome mugger can shake our confidence.

The point is that you will have as many "selves" as are required by the different roles that you play in a day, or in a lifetime.

William James also offered an interesting metaphor to prod our thinking about this. People these days sometimes go in search of their "real" selves. James suggested that looking for the self is a bit like peeling an onion. You can remove layer after layer. In the end, there is nothing there.

There is no "self" that is independent of the many roles you will play today and in your lifetime. You *are* the roles you play. Others will judge you. And it is most frequently the case that how they judge your performance in those roles will define who you "are."

We "audition" for this or that role. It is the others around us who judge our auditions. If they cast us in this or that role, we are now who we "are"—in that role.

If someone falls out of love with you, it's likely that not even the most superior job of auditioning will win back the role you lost. It's always that we perform to others' satisfaction the roles we would like to have. This is what auditioning is all about. It is always others who have the final say.

You may have "great expectations." But you can't play a role others won't endorse—whether as a leader, a lover, or a louse. Things may happen. But it is historians who connect the dots. You may be in your own mind a shaker and a mover. But if the others who pass judgment on you don't see you that way, that will not be your legacy.

You have to create who you are within the constraints that others impose upon you and that you choose—inadvertently or on purpose—for yourself, and are capable of realizing out of your fantasies.

Some years back, the American sociologist Erving Goffman wrote a book entitled *The Presentation of Self in Everyday Life*. He pointed out that we have as many selves as the roles we play in life. But what he provoked was the understanding that life is a performing art: that we *become* the roles that we perform. And that the better we choose the right ones, the better our lives could be.

We will revisit this key idea near the end of this book.

Self-Deception

What has come to be called "self-deception" raises an intriguing dilemma.

If who we imagine we are is acceptably consistent with who others imagine us to be, we are in sync with those around us. But if you intend to be someone other than you are seen to be by others, there is a conflict.

That conflict can only be reconciled by adapting to others' perceptions, or by changing their beliefs about who you are. Most people take the first, the easy path.

There is an old saying that you should take great care about whom you pretend to be. You might get the role. What's fascinating about this is that how we perform our roles determines who we will be—not the other way around. So if you want to be someone other than who you believe yourself to be, you have to *perform* your way into that other state of existence.

This implies, of course, that you have to perform your way *out* of your present way of being. In other words, you have to cease being who you are while at the same time be auditioning to be seen by others as someone other than who you are—or were—in their minds.

If you want to do life as you would have it done, you first have to convince yourself, and then convince others.

IF you would do life according to how you would have it:

- In every encounter—with yourself or with others—you have to perform yourself *out of* who you "are" and
- Simultaneously perform yourself *into* how you want others to perceive you.

Given the hold that our myriad habits have on us, this is a very difficult, tricky thing to do. For most people, that path is too ominous. It's easier just to float through life while finding acquaintances to exchange complaints about your life and theirs.

There are two basic forms of self-deception.

One occurs when you fail to have an accurate perception of how others see you and or what they expect of you. They won't tell you. You have to deduce from what they say or do how they perceive you. They often can't say. They didn't develop their perception of you on purpose. They pick it up by something akin to osmosis.

The other occurs when you have unrealized fantasies about who you are—when what you think you are does not jibe with how you perform yourself.

Andre Gide mused—

> *"It is better to be hated for what you are than loved for what you are not."*

The way we "present" ourselves may be inconsistent with who we are. If we deceive others about who we are, we have deceived ourselves.

Demosthenes was considered to be the greatest of the Greek orators. In the 3rd-century B.C. he wrote,

> *"Nothing is as easy as deceiving yourself, for what you wish you readily believe."*

Self-deception comes from taking your fantasies about yourself as reality, and acting on those wishful beliefs. People who become too "full of themselves" suffer from this failing. They are mistaking their inner fantasies about who they are for who they actually are as perceived by others in the outer world.

Self-deception could be harmless. But it isn't. Thomas Carlyle, the well-known Scottish man of letters and the author of *On Heroes, Hero-Worship, and the Heroic in History* (1841), wrote:

> *"Self-deception once yielded to, all other deceptions follow naturally more and more."*

Self-deception opens the door to deceiving others without compunction. One becomes a social chameleon, taking on the colors and the demeanor of whatever circumstances one finds oneself in. It is consistency in various circumstances that we label "character."

The lesson for doing life as you would have it done:

> First "Know Thyself," as the Oracle at Delphi blankly
> stated. This is a matter of knowing two things: how
> others perceive you, and what you should be. You
> can't do the one without doing the other. If you
> deceive yourself about either of these, you cannot
> be successful at either.

Self-Centered

People are of necessity self-centered. They must see the world—and themselves in it—from the perspective of their own minds. There is no alternative. In this respect, you *are* the center of the universe.

Still, the mind you have was produced for the most part by others. You are indebted to those others for who you are in your own mind. We cannot live self-consciously apart from those who preceded us and those who surround us. We live in a culture of inventing ourselves, and all else. That trove of prescriptions and proscriptions are what people use to audit their own behavior, and that of others.

What we consider civility—the rules of getting along with others—is largely a matter of "de-centering" oneself. Minimally, what this requires is opening yourself to the possibility that there are other minds out there. And that no two minds see things in exactly the same way. And that those other minds have just as much right to their proclivities and foibles as you do to yours.

"De-centering" yourself requires you to understand that your take on life is a conglomeration of your own interpretations colored by those of the culture and the particular subcultures you belong to. A computer programmer does not see the world as a professional athlete does. A physician does not see the world as his or her patient does.

To collaborate at all in a society—whether in a casual conversation or a life and death situation—you have to see the world as others see it. Defensive driving is a matter of calculating what the other driver might or might not do.

The insightful novelist John Updike wrote "Closing Words" in his memoirs in 1980:

> *"We feel safe, huddled within human institutions—churches, banks, madrigal groups—but these concoctions melt away at the basic moment. The self's responsibility, then, is to achieve rapport if not rapture with the giant, cosmic other: to appreciate, let's say, the walk back from the mailbox."*

Updike wrote with immense irony and indirection. He always sought to make his point obliquely—leaving it to the reader to decide what he meant by what he wrote. If we exercise that license here, we might conclude that what he meant was simply that daily life is mostly mundane. If you are not de-centered, you might not appreciate, let's say, the smell of the roses.

That fragrance emerges from outside of you. If you are centered within yourself (which is sheltered by all those human institutions) you may miss the richness that exists outside of your petty concerns.

It's as if you lived in a private castle. Your moat is intended to fend off anything that is not going on within your castle, so that you can be secure and content within yourself. Your enemies will consider this your weakness. And the world will not care one way or the other.

Thomas Fuller, whose wit we have encountered before, was an 18th-century clergyman and antiquarian. He once observed:

> *"Few men will be better than their interest bids them."*

If your "interest" is primarily yourself, you will never do in the world anything better than who you are.

Doing life as you would have it done requires you to have an "interest" or a purpose in life that is larger than you are. It requires you to "de-center" yourself—to make yourself in the image of the best that has ever been thought or done by others. It requires you to take the high road by being open to what is required to get there.

It requires you to grow yourself in the best way possible. And this requires recruiting the best minds of others in your quest. Being "right" without knowing why will not do. Being self-satisfied will not do.

As the same Thomas Fuller observed:

> *"If you love yourself too much, nobody else will love you at all."*

That may be the last word on being self-centered, and the implication for what one ought to do about it. Actually loving another—or even aspects of the world we live in—requires de-centering if it is to be efficacious. There is a sense in which doing life successfully is figuring out how and when and with whom to be "de-centered."

Who You Aren't

You are not who you think you are. You are who others think you are. Without that self-correcting loop into the real world, you are merely a victim of who you imagine you are.

You cannot be someone others will not enable or permit you to be. You cannot purposefully become someone you cannot imagine. You cannot purposefully become someone you are not capable of being. You cannot become someone who has no relevance to others. You cannot become a person who is incapable of explaining himself or herself to others.

In every culture, there are standardized roles. There are "mothers" and "fathers" and dozens of other labels for family and kin. There are "teachers" and there are "students." There are "cops" and "robbers." Even people who are labeled "insane" have to turn in a credible performance of insanity in order to get the role.

In a closed society (a primitive or "traditional" society) there were few roles. To be someone, you had to be fitted into one or another of those roles.

In an open society (a modern or evolving society) you are free to experiment with new or hybrid roles. The ones that work become possibilities for the next generation.

Some roles used to be considered taboo. Not in a "modern" society. If you can make it work, you can play any role you can imagine. It comes down to a matter of who "buys" your performance—that is, of how convincingly you can influence others to accept the variant or the rogue role you perform.

The speedier these rogue roles emerge, the less understanding of how they *should be* played. It becomes a game that has no rules beyond that of being accepted by a permissive culture.

There is a Jewish saying:

> *"When a rogue kisses you, count your teeth."*

The more roles there are, the more roles there will be. It is no coincidence that we believe in an infinitely-expanding universe. We are all victims because we are all victimizers.

Doing life as you would have it done in this world of ours is both easier and more impossible. For most people, it is a matter of innovating by emulating. We become more different by becoming more of the same. You may exaggerate your performance of your role, but the din of others clamoring for attention may limit your voice.

The "noise" may exceed the "signal." When there is free-for-all performance but no standards, there is a sense of anomie—of being adrift with no anchor. When egos run amok, the society disintegrates. When everyone decides for themselves, there is the freedom of uncertainty.

This makes doing life much easier, but without consequence. In such circumstances, as our satirical journalist Evan Esar put it,

> *"Don't be yourself—be what you ought to be."*

If you would do life as you would have it done, do not skip this step.

The famous American anthropologist Margaret Mead gave us something additionally to chew on. She wrote:

"Always remember that you are absolutely unique.
Just like everyone else."

When you try to differentiate yourself by appearance—increasingly the only discriminator in common—you may *appear* to be unique. But when everyone else is using this as evidence of who they are, you appear to be just like everyone else—with a different hairdo or jeans that have holes in different places.

To do life as you would have it done, you need some discriminator other than outward appearance. You need to have a purpose in life—and the character to go with it—that sets you apart. In spite of widespread belief to the contrary, outward appearances won't do it. You have to be, within yourself, different.

And that requires courage, commitment, and meaningful engagement with what is relevant in the world. Or, making yourself relevant in some way, large or small, to that world.

XIII

. . . Feelings: Causing and Being Caused

*"The thoughts they had were the parents of
the actions they did; their feelings were
parents of their thoughts."*

—Thomas Carlyle

People assume far more rationality in the world than actually exists. Some even assume that people's motives derive from their thoughts rather than their feelings.

Facts matter little where feelings determine beliefs, perceptions, and opinions. And that is most often the case. *We think with our feelings.* We concern ourselves with what we attend to not out of rational judgment, but because our feelings so dictate.

Whether you like someone or not depends upon how you *feel* about them. You did not arrive at the wine you like or the music you like by any careful consideration. You arrived at your preferences because your feelings about them took you there.

It isn't merely that "emotions" play a role in your life. It is that your feelings about things determine your life. We are led by our feelings about things. We relate to people and things and happenings according to how we "feel" about them.

As Carlyle suggested (above), feelings produce and channel our thoughts, *not the other way around.* It may be that how we think about things determines what we do about them. But how we think about them is not determined by those things as such, but by how we *feel* about those things.

The scholar and rhetorician James Miller wrote as follows in his 1972 book, *Word, Self, Reality: The Rhetoric of Imagination*:

> *"It is feeling that shapes belief and forms opinion. It is feeling that directs the strategy of argument. It is our feelings, then, with which we must come to . . . terms."*

"Argument" here refers to all statements and responses in even the most casual conversation. We imagine we are talking about specific events and specific immutable people when we talk with others. We are not. We are talking about our feelings about those people and those happenings.

To do life as you would have it done requires you to know that others—like you yourself—are talking from their feelings about this or that. That's why you are not and that's why they are not receptive to a rational argument. To the extent feelings are not rational, they are not amenable to rational attack. If you try to attack others' positions with "facts," they will turn defensive. So do you.

Most arguments and differences of opinion stem from different feelings. The "facts" of the case are usually irrelevant.

What does it mean to come to terms with feelings?

The meanings of things—to us—have for the most part been arrived at by feelings, not by facts. There is no right and wrong where feelings are concerned, as there might be with "facts." They are a part of us and not of the world outside of us. They therefore take precedence.

Knowing that the world turns on feelings and not on facts can be used to great advantage in doing life as you would have it done. Who is "right" and who is "wrong" are irrelevant. It is how people *feel* about things that matters to them—just as it is for you.

A belief—like an opinion—is based on feelings, not on facts. It's an age-old argument that persists today. Why won't people listen to reason? Why do people believe things that cannot be proved one way or the other? Most people do not live by reason and by rationality.

If you assume they do, you are the one who is out of step. "Coming to terms" with the core of how we think and do requires you to make peace with that core: that people think and act according to their feelings. After all, you do.

Opinions—at Work and in Play

Differing opinions are the chief cause of people's problems with one another. We *work* at getting others to see the world as we do. But what's in play as the confrontations ramp up is not actually what we presume to be talking about. What is unavoidably in play is how differently we *feel* about those things.

The well-known 19th-century evolutionary philosopher Herbert Spencer had this to say about how opinions are determined by feelings:

> *"Opinion is ultimately determined by the feelings, and not by the intellect."*

We do not need an opinion and then think our way into it. We have feelings about everything that is meaningful to us. And these feelings produce our opinions about those things.

It is pragmatically useful to speculate on the proposition that opinions precede facts, and that we invent the facts needed to support our opinions. This is intriguingly related to what Einstein said about facts and theories (paraphrased):

> *Theories are required to gather facts. There are no facts except as they relate to the theories we hold to be true.*

Our theories (or our opinions) are like the nets we use to capture facts. We wouldn't know what facts we are looking for if we didn't have an opinion that might need them.

Another useful angle on this is provided by the 17th-century aphorist La Rochefoucauld:

"Unless they share our opinions, we seldom find
people sensible."

We are predisposed not to understand people who do not share our opinions, and to understand without skepticism people who do share our opinions. People who do not see the world as we do are not "sensible" to us. Those who do see the world with the same opinions we have become our friends.

People who share opinions constitute a network (of friends or close acquaintances). Those who are not of the same opinion are likely to be excluded as misguided or simply "wrong" about the things for which we have the strongest opinions.

There is "popular" opinion. That arises from a common need to think like the people you talk to most often think, aided and abetted by the media pap they collectively imbibe. But someone or something has to tell us what to think, what to have, what to feel, what to do or say. Thus popular opinion becomes the culture we look to for the prescriptions and proscriptions of the day. They congeal around the need people have to be in step with the fashions of the day, to "keep up with the Joneses," whoever "the Joneses" may be for you today.

Popular opinion, and the bulk of it pop psychology, is what people dip into in lieu of thinking. When thinking becomes a lost art, there is always popular opinion to provide a substitute.

Public opinion works in much the same way—except that it is molded by clever journalists and "experts" of all stripes. It is public opinion that influences our government policies and laws. It is more manufactured than revealed. So it functions much as our private opinions function for choosing up sides for agreement or disagreement.

In an address to the Associated Press in 1915, Woodrow Wilson said to them:

"You deal in the raw material of opinion, and, if my
convictions have any validity, opinion ultimately
governs the world."

Opinion certainly governs the world we personally inhabit, and thus the course of our lives. Our opinions govern us. Doing life as you would have it done will require you to choose carefully the opinions that will underlie the course you hope to take.

If the governance of your own life depends upon the popular opinions of the day, you will be molded by those opinions. They are either chosen or not. You cannot do life as you would have it done if you do not choose the ones you need.

The German poet and essayist Heinrich Heine wrote (in 1837):

> *"People in those old times had convictions; we moderns*
> *only have opinions. And it needs more than a mere*
> *opinion to erect a Gothic cathedral."*

In using that exemplar, Heine is saying that opinions cannot raise great human accomplishments for us to admire—whether these be in art or in science or in business. Those require depth of thought and a willingness to be wrong. We often use opinions to keep us from the risk of thinking for ourselves. But thinking for ourselves is not an easy thing to do in this modern world of ours. Doing so requires depth and breadth and the courage of one's hard-won convictions. They require study and effort.

Although Heine was talking about Savoye, appointed ambassador to Frankfurt in1848, he could have been talking about anyone who slavishly follows popular opinion:

> *"Ordinarily he is insane, but he has lucid moments*
> *when he is only stupid."*

To go where popular opinion leads us may be seen as a form of sanity. But it does obscure the fact that we may only be stupid.

The point is that popular opinion will only take you where popular opinion leads. Unless you choose your fate in that irresponsible way, you have to make the effort to do your own life as it should be done.

It was our homespun philosopher and printer Elbert Hubbard who averred (in 1923):

> *"Public opinion is the judgment of the incapable*
> *many opposed to that of the discerning few."*

Doing life as you would have it done requires you to be one of the discerning few.

What *Causes* You to Feel This Way or That?

In other words, what justifies your feelings? How do you explain to yourself or to others why you feel the way you do?

If you were the only person on earth, you *might* have certain human-like feelings. But if you couldn't talk about them, of what use would they be to you?

In every culture and in every subculture (including a two-person relationship), there are algorithms for understanding why you feel the way you do, and for explaining that to others.

If your feelings can't be justified by others, they won't be recognized.

In the film *When Harry Met Sally*, the two of them are together on a cross-country road trip—for complex reasons. They stop at a diner. The conversation turns to faking orgasms. He said it couldn't happen to him. He would know. So she proceeds to fake an orgasm while seated at their table. He is astonished. A woman at the next booth, who had been observing, said, "I'll have what she's having"—which could have a double meaning.

The key point here is that feelings are totally private. No one can see or experience your feelings. They can enter the public domain only by how you express this or that feeling. You audition to "have" a certain feeling. If you convince others by how you express yourself, you get the part.

The world turns on performance, not on thoughts or feelings or beliefs as such.

As the famous art and social critic John Ruskin put it thus:

> *"What we think or what we know or what we believe is,*
> *in the end, of little consequence. The only thing of*
> *consequence is what we do."*

Any feeling you might "have"—and who would know but you?—are of little consequence. The only thing of consequence is how you express them or perform them.

So, back to Harry and Sally. He will either believe her performance, determine her performance to be without validity, or try otherwise to get to the "truth" of the matter.

Write off the third course of reaction. You cannot determine the "truth" of anything except by performing it. If he doesn't buy her faking, he loses. If he does, life can go on.

We have to take such things on faith. You either believe it or you don't. If you do, life goes on. If you don't, life takes a different path.

The same kind of situation was reprised in a *Seinfeld* segment. Jerry was sure that Elaine had many great orgasms when they were a couple. Like Harry, he would know. She said "No, all fakes." "All of them?" he asks. "All of them," she replies. "Give me another chance," he says. The male ego is at risk here.

What all of this says to us is simple enough. What exists in the privacy of our own minds or our own hearts or bodies plays no part in the real world. The world turns on how we perform ourselves in it.

This opens wide the door to being duped. The other person is auditioning. You are guessing what it means—whether to "buy" it or not. Suppose a person offers you a hearty handshake. Your inclination may be to decide that this is a sincere person. That's what makes you dupable. People will try all sorts of performance maneuvers in order to get the best of you. And you have no certain way of knowing.

Your physician may ask you how you feel. But he looks at the lab report and the charts to qualify your answer. Since there is no lab test for "love," you have to go on faith. You could go on performance. But performing *any* feelings or ailments can be faked.

In one very important sense, what *causes* our feelings is performing them. Who is to say a faked orgasm might not be better than a real one?

If you want to be seen as depressed, for example, you have to practice your performance as a depressed person. You have to learn the clues and the symptoms and perform them convincingly. Your friends will help with this. So will the media. We are confronted with far more images of how to audition as a person who has this or that ailment than with images of robust good health. What turns us on, apparently, is the bad things we might "have." But to have them in the eyes of others, we still have to audition successfully.

We live in a culture that perniciously encourages ailments of mind and body. We are expected to have problems. If we didn't, what would we talk to others about socially?

Doing life as you should do it requires you to take the high road. As W.C. Fields once remarked, *"Trust everybody. But cut the cards."* Take people at face value. But let chance play its role. Don't swallow any performance whole. Ask questions. They are the best defense you have.

The flip side can be derived from a comment made by Eleanor Roosevelt, about which she felt very strongly:

> *"No one can make you feel inferior without your consent."*

She is pointing out that, for example, prejudice is a two-way street. Those who feel they are victims of prejudice often want to keep the feeling going because, in some perverse way, it serves their interests.

Even more so, she is suggesting that no one can make you feel . . . anything . . . without your consent. At least, that is the position to be taken by anyone who intends to do life well by having a purpose in life. No one can "make" you feel sad or glad or happy or despondent or irritated or pleased—without your complicity. What this means is that you must manage your own feelings, not be "made" to have them by other people or by the happenings of the day.

There is nothing in a slur made by another person that obligates you to feel offended. You are not obligated to be "caused" to have any of the currently popular feelings just because the culture gives you a justification for being so.

What *Causes* You to Have the Feelings that Overtake You?

In our culture, particularly, we like to believe that the feelings we have are caused by the people or the events of our lives. We like to be able to say, "You make (or that makes) me angry." Or that "This organization (or this relationship) doesn't make me happy any more." Or that "It really pisses me off when that happens!"

We prefer to attribute our good feelings to ourselves, our bad feelings to others or to happenings over which we have no control.

Here's where you can do some really valuable groundwork on your project of doing life.

If you are vulnerable to the feelings that are "going around" (or that other people want to infect you with), you have what might be called *hot buttons*. If they are detected, someone will push them. They may do it inadvertently. They may do it just because they can. They may do it because they delight in your reactions. They may do it in order to have a sense of power over you. They may do it just to be entertained by your going ballistic.

If certain things irritate you, you can be assured that you will bump up against them. If your feelings are the effect, you can be certain that the cause will occur. It is, in a sense, invited. Whatever you are susceptible to with respect to your feelings will find its way to you.

If you do not want to be this kind of puppet or punching bag, there is only one preventative:

Have no "hot buttons," or at least none that are perceptible
to those people who have little else to do but push others'
hot buttons.

Anyone who has a cause in their own lives will have to train themselves to be impervious to others who would push their hot buttons. Do not seduce others through their hot buttons. Ignore their hot buttons. This will help you to avoid being seduced by others who for no good reason push your hot buttons.

In other words, be discriminately susceptible—be susceptible only to those people whose influence will aid your cause in life. Be discriminately seductive—seduce only those who can be greatly aided by your seduction of them.

Do not be "caused" by love or hate or idolization. Have
a cause that is loftier than these. Have the kind of greater
cause that makes you immune to petty provocations—
even your own.

To avoid being deceived, never be a deceiver. Doing life as you would have it done requires you to be above the feeling games that people play. Do not succumb to feelings that make no contribution to your cause in life. Do not permit anyone around you to succumb to feelings that will not serve their best self-interests.

Feelings are inescapable. In every life, they are ubiquitous. You just have to choose those that are beneficial and avoid those that are detrimental.

If you have a worthy cause in life, you will know what those are.

Be neither the causer of feelings detrimental to others, nor be caused by feelings that do not grow you in spirit and character.

Desire and Satiation

We all have "desires." Most of these are socially created, perpetuated by the media. What we desire is what we are supposed to desire—because the thing or the person or the place is . . . desirable.

But, note well:

- A desire once sated or outgrown no longer exists.

- An appetite once sated or displaced no longer exists.

- A lust once sated or neglected no longer exists.

- An anger once exhausted no longer exists.

- A pleasure once over-exploited no longer exists.

Feelings do not exist before they are enacted and thus recognized. When they have served their temporary purposes, they return to whence they came—from nowhere to nowhere.

They may be the drivers of our thinking and our opinions. But they are unreliable motives. They take us where *they* go, not where we should be going.

Doing life as you would have it done requires you to choose and to manage your feelings.

We dealt with "Causes and Consequences" in an earlier chapter. If those do not dovetail perfectly with what we have raised here, go back and look at that chapter again.

Causes have consequences. However you explain your feelings, it is the consequences they bring upon you that you have to look out for.

In James Boswell's *Life of Samuel Johnson* (1783), Samuel Foote is given to comment on a dull law lord:

"He is not only dull in himself, but the cause of dullness in others."

Like feelings, dullness is contagious. Doing life as it should be done requires that you immunize yourself against wayward contagion and thoughtless acting out.

XIV

. . . Regret and Forgiveness

"My only regret in the theatre is that I could never sit out front and watch me."

—John Barrymore (attrib.)

Life is full of pain and pleasure, regret, forgiveness, and just plain banality. We have a pop culture that encourages people to have pie-in-the-sky hopes and dreams. It doesn't much offer the reality that most of these will never come to pass. They will almost never come to pass because they exist primarily in our imaginations.

There are all kinds of recipes you can buy for realizing your dreams. But it is almost exclusively the purveyors of these recipes that reap benefits. You can't look like the air-brushed models who happen to be beautiful unless you are an airbrushed model who happens to be beautiful. No one tells you that you can't get there unless you genetically have the potential. And that you would still need a lot of luck on top of a lot of pain and effort.

All you need to become a rich CEO is a book that tells you how. All you need to have a happy life is a seminar that tells you how. Love stories are still the most purchased, the least lived as told.

You can certainly buy what you are told you need in order to remedy any situation, or to achieve your hopes and dreams. The only problem is that you can't *buy* the life you envision. You have to make it. And that requires your diligence and your dedication. There is no fairy-dust that will do it for you.

What You *Should Have* and *Shouldn't Have* Done

All regret is retrospective. We observe it and generate our feelings by looking at something in the past as if in a rear-view mirror.

There are probably four different kinds of regret:

- Regret for doing or saying something you now feel you shouldn't have.

- Regret for not doing or saying something you now feel you should have.

- Regret for not doing or saying something that you could have.

- Regret for not doing or saying something that you *would* have, if it hadn't been for the circumstances as you remember them.

Every kind of regret—and the feelings that attend it—is generated by one's *conscience*. People who have weak or non-existent consciences feel no regret. Those who have powerful moral consciences are the ones who suffer from regret.

A person who has no conscience might regret not having killed an adversary when he or she had the opportunity to do so. But there is not much in the way of feelings connected to that kind of regret.

For people with fully-functioning consciences, regret is punitive: they accuse themselves and punish themselves internally for what they should have done, or should not have done. If their regret is grievous, they may even obsess over it.

The New Zealand-born writer Katherine Mansfield commented:

> *"Regret is an appalling waste of time; you can't build on it;*
> *it's only good for wallowing in."*

For those who are keen on doing life as they would have it done, here's the lesson:

Do not waste your time wallowing in regret. You can't change your life by feeling regretful. There is nothing constructive in it. What's done is proverbial "spilt milk."

Still, the question is: How to avoid participating in what is almost a universal game akin to solitaire? It's easy to say don't do it. But it's harder to avoid such a widespread custom seemingly engaged in by everyone else.

When you don't know anyone who doesn't regret *something*, how are you to forge your own path in life?

The 20th-century Nobel Prize-winning German writer Elias Canetti offered us these questions in his book *The Human Province*:

"One man says he can regret nothing. A god? A stone?"

This is intended to point out the universality of modern human engagement in regret. If you think of yourself as acceding to the norms of society, then you will feel regret, like all the rest of us. Yet it may be, as Mansfield wrote, an appalling waste of time.

What is normative in a given culture both enables certain feelings and actions, and constrains others. If feeling regret is normative, how can it be wrong?

When you make a choice and act on it, you put yourself on a path defined by that choice. So there is always the question, "What if I had taken another path?" "Might I have had a better life if I had made a different choice back then?"

This you can never know because you didn't take that other path in your life. There are no dress rehearsals for doing life. You can't go back and do it differently. What's done can't be undone. What wasn't done back then can't be done. That's all in the past.

Therein lies the dilemma for doing life. The choices you made in the past put you where you are today. The choices you make today will put you where you will be in the future. You can't change the choices you made in the past. And the choices you make today will not *guarantee* the life you want tomorrow.

But life is a journey, not a destination. Most people don't enjoy the endless journey. So they opt out of real life along the way.

Woody Allen, cleverly writing in the third person "About the Author" in *Getting Even* (1971) said:

> *"His one regret in life is that he is not someone else."*

Many regrets probably come down to this—that we regret not being someone else. Perhaps even more so, that we regret not being who we ought to be.

Doing life as you would have it done requires that you become that "someone else." Yet it seems that most people prefer the life they have—no matter how bad it is—over the life they could have, should have, ought to have. The pertinent old axiom is:

> *"Most people prefer a problem they can't solve to a solution they don't like."*

The old habits are stronger than wishful thinking. Add to that the fact that most people believe they don't have what it takes to execute a different path in life. The poet T. S. Eliot refers to this as

> *". . . the door we never opened . . . ."*

That's why people don't change much—because they "can't." They prefer the regret over the achievement, which strikes them as being really, really hard. They wouldn't know, of course, unless they actually made a serious and dedicated attempt to change the course of their lives.

So they—we—live vicariously, through the media-dramatized lives of those who are indeed "someone else."

The well-known pianist/humorist Oscar Levant, in an ad-libbed line spoken by himself, said:

> *"It is not what you are; it's what you don't become that hurts."*

You won't find Levant amongst the best-sellers in the self-help section of the bookstore. But that just makes the point: the wisdom you need to become different is probably not on the shelves of the best-sellers, whatever the genre. That's where the fashions of the day are.

What you don't become, hurts. If this were true, then most people would be really hurting. They are not. They may have regrets. But are more or less satisfied with their lives because they prefer the problems they have to a solution they don't like—or couldn't execute even if they did.

There is the American saying,

"Woulda, coulda, shoulda"

You won't find those slang words in the dictionary. But they seem to express the most common regrets.

One "woulda" done the right thing back then, but was busy doing something else perhaps. Or it just didn't occur to him or her.

One "coulda" said or done something that woulda made the whole thing turn out for the better. But didn't. There were some reasons why.

One "shoulda" done this or that, but didn't. There may be some degree of regret and guilt that one didn't, but there is always a good excuse, it seems.

Things usually appear more rational in retrospect. But now is not then. And then there were—weren't there?—extenuating circumstances. What a person woulda, coulda, or shoulda said or done were not subject to any rationality at the time. That only came with the retrospective and the regret.

But how is one to know at the time what he or she coulda or shoulda done? The consequences are always off in an unknown future. If we knew the outcomes, we might make better judgments. But we can't know those. And maybe the right thing to be done was not possible—personal and social limitations may have existed. Maybe we wanted to, but couldn't.

For those who want to do life as they would have it done, everything cannot be circumstantial. You have to have principles that operate in spite of the circumstances. That's what consciences are for—to preclude you from doing what you ought not, and to give you the courage to do what you ought.

By the time you regret something done or undone even in the immediate present, it is already too late. You have to start with what you *might* regret doing or not doing—and let that be your beacon. That's not an easy thing to do. But there is no other antidote.

John Greenleaf Whittier, the American abolitionist and poet (second, it was said, only to Longfellow) wrote in 1854:

> "Of all sad words of tongue or pen,
> The saddest are these: 'It might have been!'"

Words echoed by the famous English poet William Butler Yeats (in *The Winding Stair and other Poems*, 1933):

> "Things said or done long years ago,
> Or things I did not do or say
> But thought that I might say or do,
> Weigh me down, and not a day
> But something is recalled,
> My conscience or my vanity appalled."

It is often in poetry and other literature that we find such feelings as shame and regret and lost love and unhappiness so poignantly set forth.

It is not the stuff of everyday gossip. The warnings and the wisdom are there in such resources. We do not heed them because we just don't expose ourselves to them.

Doing life as one would do it probably requires this kind of literacy. It is always hidden in everyday conversations—even with oneself. It is revealed only in serious literature, such as the poem excerpts above.

Why *do* we have such a difficult time of doing life the way we even know it should be done? Why is regret such a common twinge of conscience or of "vanity"?

It's easier to do life wrong than right. It's easier yet not even to try. Living circumstantially, without conscience, is the best way of destroying both the individual and the society. Is this merely suicidal? Or is something else going on?

Forgiveness

This is a big word in the Christian psyche. We are supposed to forgive others as we forgive ourselves. The problem is, most people never learn how to forgive themselves. We seem to prefer the onus of guilt over the act of forgiveness. Why *is* that?

The 19th-century Danish philosopher and theologian Soren Kierkegaard offered us a key clue to this problem of doing life when he wrote:

> *"Life can only be understood backwards . . . but it must be lived forwards."*

It is an obvious idea—once you see it in print. And it is one we will return to again and again.

You cannot change anything in your past—although you could interpret its relevance quite differently if you chose to do so. We can understand ourselves only by looking back and interpreting our personal and collective history. But we have to live life "forwards," as Kierkegaard said.

What this implies, rather strongly, is that the only acceptable reason for dwelling on the past is to extract the lessons needed for moving forward. There is no good purpose served by wallowing in regret or guilt or shame. It is time to forgive yourself and move on.

Doing life refers solely to doing the life you envision in the future. You can't "do" life in the past. You've already done that—for better or for worse. What's required is forgiving yourself for your past mistakes and errors of omission.

You don't even need to analyze *why* you did what you did, or failed to do what you should have done. It is sufficient for you to see what part of the problem you were, fix that, and move on. We all have regrets. The aim is to have fewer of them as you move ahead toward your goals in life. You will never eliminate your errors of judgment. They will arise as long as you are alive.

And then in those last days, you will probably be struck with what the 18th-century wit Samuel Johnson observed:

> *"It is a mortifying reflection for any man to consider what*
> *he has done compared with what he might have done."*

Even those who have achieved or accomplished in towering ways have had such reflections. Achievers like Edison, Alexander the Great, or even Michelangelo suffered their dissatisfactions with what they left undone in their view of what they might have done.

So you can't ultimately escape such concerns about regret. Just do not dwell on them. You don't have time to do so. If you are going to do life as you would have it done, you have more than enough to concern you moving ahead.

The purpose of having a hard-nosed conscience is not to punish you for the way things turned out. It is to help you make things turn out as you would have them. But conscience does not rule the world. The world does. Learn from your mistakes and move on.

You will never do life perfectly. It will always turn out to be a product of you *and* of the events of that world beyond your control.

As the famous 19th-century American poet Emily Dickinson averred:

> *"Of God we ask one favor,*
> *That we may be forgiven—*
> *For what, he is presumed to know—*
> *The crime, from us, is hidden—"*

We often do not know the harm we do to others, or to the society in which we live. We may not be aware of the unintended consequences of what we say or do—or what we don't say or do. Then we need to be forgiven by a higher power, an omniscient power.

If we are unaware of the harm we do, we cannot forgive ourselves. Does it work if someone or something else does this for us? Or, if we play God ourselves, do we need to develop more cognizance of our crimes—which from us are "hidden"?

Probably the latter. If we unwittingly do harm to others—or indirectly to the society we share—those others will be reluctant to aid and abet us in doing our own lives. For that practical reason alone you may need to be more aware of your "trespasses."

Would a philosopher lie to you for his or her own benefit? Yes. So might you. George Bernard Shaw made an interesting observation. He wrote:

> *"The secret of forgiving everything is to understand nothing."*

There are things that you do (or don't do) that are essentially unforgivable in their consequences. Then it is not forgiveness that you need, but learning. You need to *understand* how you affect others and all the rest of the world. That requires learning from your "trespasses" what part of the problem you are, and avoiding the rush to forgiving yourself for everything you do—or don't do.

Pre-ordained forgiveness may not be in your best self-interests. Understanding how you might negatively affect the world around you may be more important than forgiving yourself in advance.

Nor should you preemptively forgive others for the wrong they do. The British writer W. Somerset Maugham turns the whole process on its head in the following:

> *"People will sometimes forgive you the good you have done them, but seldom the harm they have done you."*

Is he saying that people may not forgive *you* for the harm they have done you? But that they will sometimes forgive you the good you have done them?

In this perverse sort of way, he is reminding us that "good" and "harm" are both in the eye of the beholder. Your attempt to do good for people may be resented by them. They may see your actions or your words as attempts to be superior to them. No matter that was not what you intended.

You may interpret the harm they have done you as an attempt on their part to do you good. Can you forgive their misinterpretations? Can you forgive your own misinterpretations?

The reason for forgiveness cannot rest entirely on intention. There are always unintended consequences. And those unintended consequences may come from how you—or they—interpret what you did, or did not do.
You may intend well. But if you are incompetent to *do* well, should you be forgiven for your incompetence? Or would it be better to *understand* what is going on, as Shaw suggested?

There are those who would argue that understanding is the *same* thing as forgiving. But our understandings—our interpretations—are always imperfect. So perhaps Shaw was right: when we substitute forgiveness for understanding, it may not be an unmitigated good.

Maybe the only thing to regret is one's failure to *learn* from the consequences of what is done or what is not. If so, then forgiveness is a matter of doing a better job of learning how you impact the world and how the world impacts you.

> With others, you get what you tolerate. And they get
> what they tolerate. If you tolerate the harm that can
> be done to you by others, your life does not belong to
> you but to them. Can you forgive that in yourself?
> Should you?

There is as well a distinction to be made between forgiving and forgetting. Perhaps the Hungarian-born psychiatrist Thomas Szasz resolves the dilemma by making just such a distinction:

> "The stupid neither forgive nor forget; the naïve forgive and
> forget; the wise forgive but do not forget."

So this leaves the choice to you which you shall be.

And *a propos* the conundrum presented by Maugham above, we have this from Shaw:

> *"Beware of the man who does not return your blow: he*
> *neither forgives you nor allows you to forgive yourself."*

Doing life as you would have it done requires you not to be that person. People need to know who you are and why you are. Above all, they need to know what you will tolerate.

Forgiveness—either of yourself or others, when deserved—is hollow and insincere unless it is driven by principle. This is how you let people know who you are, and why.

> *"Since nothing we intend is ever faultless;*
> *and nothing we attempt ever without error;*
> *and nothing we achieve without some measure*
> *of finitude and fallibility we call humanness,*
> *we are saved by forgiveness.*

—American theologian & author David Augsburger

XV

. . . Fads and Fashions

*"Fashion, n. A despot whom the wise ridicule
and obey."*

—Ambrose Bierce (*The Devil's Dictionary*, 1911)

"Fashions, after all, are only induced epidemics."

—George Bernard Shaw, in *The Doctor's
Dilemma* (1906)

There was a time when people were tyrannized by *tradition*. In the modern, hyper-connected world, we are tyrannized not by tradition, but by fashion. You can't be "in" unless you are in fashion with those of the circles in which you move.

We are here not discussing "high fashion," or even fashions in clothes. We will want to come to terms with the fact that fashions tyrannize us in all aspects of life—how we think, how we feel, what we drive, what we eat, how we choose a friend or a spouse, house or a neighborhood, the illnesses we have and the treatments we seek, and how we look in the mirror and how we comport ourselves in public.

We have what might be termed a "social conscience." We want to be seen by others in a certain way. Whether in the office or the restaurant, we want the others of the crowds we move in to attribute to us the persona we are trying to broadcast.

Our first and compelling thoughts are, "How will others judge me?" "If I say this or do that, how will other people pass judgment on me?" "Will I gain or lose social capital if I live in this sort of house or travel to this sort of place?"

There was a time—still is in some cultures—when most things were dictated by tradition. But, as Goethe wrote:

"What is called fashion is the tradition of the moment."

It is just as tyrannical. Almost everything you do or say or think or feel or have is guided by fashion—the tradition of the moment in your circle of friends and acquaintances. You even want to be "in" and awarded social capital by people you don't know or may never see again.

We touched upon the subject before, in a different context. Here we will want to delve deeply into this pervasive condition of our lives. If you are committed to doing life as you would have it done, you need to have a real "feel" for what's at stake.

If you're normal, for example, you are like a puppet, and the strings are the pushes and pulls of fashion—of the tradition of the moment. You are more likely under the yoke of the social protocols of the day than of your own private thoughts. What you say is more likely to be what "people" say in such-and-such a situation than what you really wanted to say.

We will talk to others about the celebrities we share. We will talk about the "news," and of the TV shows we share. We will talk about what we did—which will be essentially what "everybody" else did that day or yesterday. If you talk ideas, they will likely be the ideas of the day. They will have been promulgated by the gurus, experts, or media celebrities of the day.

Our syndicated columnist/satirist Evan Esar had an interesting observation. He wrote:

"Many a man smiles at his wife for slavishly following the fashions of dress while he is slavishly following the fashions in thought."

This is why our current buildings look so much alike. This is why most CEOs and politicians sound so much alike. This is why professors think like academics and plumbers think like plumbers. This is why diet fads come and go. This is why advertisers copy each other. This is why even you may wear clothes that are in fashion, or are at least not "out" of fashion.

So what was Shaw suggesting when he said that fashions are induced epidemics?

The Origin and the Destination of Fashions

Fashions—in thought and feelings and opinions as well, remember—seem to be anonymous. They are not. But how they gain traction with large numbers of people can't really be deciphered. They can be traced (somewhat) and "explained" after the fact. But they cannot be predicted.

Most conditions of thought and feeling, or of dress and comportment that could become fashions of the day do not become the fashions of the day.

Only a tiny percentage of all of the possibilities ever become serious contenders.

Even conscious attempts to create a mass fashion fail far more than they succeed. Consider the fashion designers or automobile designers. Some people might like to BE Oprah. But they won't be. She was an anomaly.

Widespread fashions of any sort come from anomalies. It is the theorist in some field of science who proposes a new theory of something. That theory is an anomaly in the context of the older, reigning theories. It may first be ridiculed. But when larger numbers of one's peers gather around it, it gets considered and may gain traction amongst scientists and others in general. It may become a general belief—as in "evolution," for example.

But we know that the theories of the day are a sort of fashion. That's because they will be eclipsed by a newer theory. Theories or beliefs or opinions of the day are fashionable. They are fashionable or they are ignored and forgotten.

Kim Campbell, the Canadian Prime Minister back in the 90's is quoted as saying:

"Does fashion matter? Only if you're out of it."

There is no particular payoff for being "in" fashion. It is what's expected. But there is a subtle and pernicious punishment for being "out" of fashion. People *will* talk behind your back if you appear to be out of step with what is fashionable.

Epidemiology is a complex of procedures to be followed when one wants to study the emergence, spread, and control of a disease or some other condition related to health. It is probably the best model we have for studying the emergence and spread of fashions.

Where do fashions go when they are superseded? To the same place they existed before they emerged—from possibilities to the archives. A look back at photos taken in even the past century will make it clear that fashions—even in facial expressions—come and go. They come out of "nowhere" and more often sooner than later disappear to the same place.

Fashions Are "Contagious"

Fashions are contagious. Not in the biological sense. Fashions are "contagious" for the following reasons:

- People are notorious imitators, as in "Monkey see, monkey do." People who live in a tribe are more like one another than like those who are not in their tribe. Plumbers are more likely to think like and comport themselves like other plumbers than like musicians or sports stars or politicians. That's another proverb: "Birds of a feather flock together." Except for humans, it's more likely to be the other way around: "Birds that flock together end up having the same kind of feathers."

- We have two ways of being "contagious": one of course is biological. The other is communicative. If you are open to what others say or do, they are *colonizing* your mind. If they are open to what you say or do, you are colonizing their minds. It is the mind and its habits that run the show. If we are going to communicate comfortably with others, it is because our minds are at least minimally "synchronized." If what we are doing is time-sensitive, we have to synchronize our watches. It won't work if the other person thinks idiosyncratically (or whose "watch" is not set at the same time yours is).

- People have to think more or less alike to be able to communicate with one another comfortably. And people have to be in regular communication with one another to think more or less alike. It is unlikely that you could ever become close friends with a person whose mind didn't function reasonably well like yours does.

- You were not born with the mind you have today. Your mind was born in communication to and from others. It exists today in communication to and from others. The "contents" and the processes of your mind were born in and get maintained daily in communication to and from others. This is what makes us *contagious*.

- Small children like other children who are most like them. If you don't think and believe like I do, we may have to go to war to settle our differences. If we "fall in love," it needs to be mutual. If we fall out of love, it needn't be mutual. We are often attracted to others according to how much of ourselves we see in them—and vice versa. Others, in how much of themselves they see in us. In other words, if someone else sees you like you would hope to be seen, you like them. If you see them as they would hope to be seen, they like you. Those you don't feel compatible with, you ostracize. Those who do not feel compatible with the ways you think and do ostracize you. By expressing ourselves as clichés, we become clichés.

- When we talk to others (mediated or not), we are colonizing their minds. When others talk to us (mediated or not), they are colonizing our minds. If they are mentally deranged (i.e., not "normal" like the rest of us)—as in the film, *Don Juan DeMarco*—we are inclined to lock them away. But if we talk with them long enough (as the psychiatrist did), we begin to see the world the way they do.

- The contagious part is simply that—if we "understand" what others are saying or doing, our minds are thereby infected. Those we have no communication with are no threat to us. But those with whom we are most often in communication will most infect us, and we them. That is the concern about commercial television. People generally are more in communication with the media than with other people directly. We come to think like the commercial advertisers would like us to think. Heavy consumers of TV fare begin to feel more like the characters they encounter in their "favorite" shows than like their neighbors.

We come to think like others, to comport ourselves as they do, to live in houses that are like theirs, to dress and coif ourselves like they do, to vacation in the same spots they do, and to have the same illnesses and sports (or other) addictions they do. Where there is a "mass market" for advertising or for TV programs, that means we—you—have become a part of the "mass."

We live—in our minds and our feelings, our doing and our undoing—in the flurry of epidemics (and pandemics) that swirl around us.

The most pernicious obstacle to doing life as you would do your life—is there. If having your mind colonized by whatever is going around suits you, then you will be fine. If that is not the case, you have some changes to make.

People didn't get divorced so often before it became popular to do so. People didn't have premarital sex (openly) until it became popular to do so. Everything you know and know how to do came to you because you were susceptible to it—you had no immunity to it.

We can safely alter Shaw's epigram (at the top of this chapter) by acknowledging that the epidemics of fashion of which he spoke afflict people differently. Some people are more susceptible than others. Some people are more immune than others. It is selective susceptibility and selective immunity to the contagious world of beliefs and images and narratives that you seek.

All of your thinking, doing, saying, having, and ways of being will depend upon how you permit your mind to be colonized. Contagion may be imperceptible. But it can only

happen with your tacit permission. It is tacit because you
have certain susceptibilities and certain immunities.

There is your adversary. People wouldn't relate to one
another or become disenchanted with one another in the
ways they do if it were not popular (imaginable or somehow
necessary for them) to do so. Maybe they saw it on TV.
Maybe most of their friends are behaving that way.

What is normative easily becomes a habit. And habits drive
you where they go—not necessarily where you want *to go.*

Neither Words nor Kisses Define Themselves

Whatever you are capable of being conscious of is meaningful to you—in one way or another.

Consciousness and meaning are two aspects of the same thing. What things mean to you direct your consciousness. The world you live in is a world of the meaning of things. The things are whatever they are. It is how they mean to *you* that brings you into contact with them. Your contact or understanding of them comes from what they mean *to you*.

So, as above—

Neither words nor kisses define themselves.

You define them. They are what they mean—*to you*.

What you are susceptible to at any moment is what is most meaningful to you at that moment. What you are immune to is whatever is not meaningful to you at that moment.

You have your life in those moments—not in words or kisses, photos or touches, happenings or memories—but in what those things *mean* to you at any given moment. *You become what you pay attention to.* And you pay attention to whatever is meaningful to you at a given moment, and in whatever way it is meaningful to you.

Meanings are social constructions. They are the raw material of which your own meanings are made. Take away the meaning and you would be no more than literally conscious of what is right in front of you. You grasp the world with the mind you have to grasp it with. And your mind is in turn a product of the meanings that are at play there.

It is our own peculiar culture that enables us to say we are "looking for" the meaning of something. In the end, what we are looking for will be no more than what we make of it with our own minds at that moment.

The philosopher E. M. Cioran wrote (in his book *The New Gods*, 1969):

> *"To look for a meaning in anything is less the act of a*
> *naïf than of a masochist."*

A "naïf" is a naïve person. A masochist is a person who enjoys what appears to be painful or tiresome. So searching for the meaning of things *in* those things will end up being at least disagreeable. We can as readily impose a negative as a positive meaning—as when we fall out of love, having previously been in love. However we assign meaning to what we can't understand will be uncomfortable at best.

It is tiresome because the meaning we give to the things and happenings of our lives comes most immediately from ourselves. We give it a meaning which came from us. That is a "tiresome" activity unless you are an optimistic poet—in which case it may serve a purpose to define and redefine things to the end of making them appear to be different from what we thought. That is, of making our meanings work for us rather than our working for them.

The 20th-century American author Henry Miller offered this (in his book, *The Wisdom of the Heart*, 1941):

> *"Life has to be given a meaning because of the obvious*
> *fact that it has no meaning."*

The operant term here is *given*. The worlds we inhabit have to be *given* whatever they mean to us. How you give meaning to the world determines not only what you will mean to yourself, but also how others will "read" you—that is, what you mean to them.

The meanings you take for granted are what differentiate you from the natural world (and the social world with all of its cacophony).

Doing any kind of life that is meaningful to you—no matter how much you approve or disapprove of it—begins here.

> You make your life out of meanings. Get those right and you have the greatest possibility of doing your life as you would have it done.

> In defining your world, you define yourself.

> That can take you where you want to go. Or it can take you straight to your personal hell, as Freud suggested.

Pain and Pleasure

No one is born knowing what pain and pleasure are. Until you learn how to experience them by expressing them, you will merely be exposed to relatively meaningless happenings in your life.

You might experience all kinds of happenings *subjectively*. But for those subjective experiences to become meaningful to others, you have to learn how to audition as having them before those other people. About such performances in public, there are always norms.

If you perform pain or pleasure successfully (think of the fake orgasm scene in *When Harry Met Sally*) in public, you are entitled to have them in this *objective* sense.

*You can **have**—now or later—the pleasure or pain you can express.*

People can only *have* the feelings of love that they can express. You can't "have" (in the eyes of others) any feelings you cannot perform acceptably. This becomes a critical factor in health and illness as well as in love.

When a physician is assessing "your" pain, much depends upon how you express it—upon how well you audition as a person in a specific level of pain compared to all other patients. Once the physician becomes mindful of your pain and talks about it, it becomes objective. It exists in the "real" world.

Thus, how it is talked about provides the parameters not only for understanding it, but for experiencing it.

It may seem perverse. But what this perspective reveals is that you will only "have" the kinds of pleasure and pain you can express. You will "have" the kinds of pains and pleasures others attribute to you.

It doesn't make much difference if you fake an orgasm or a pain. If it seems legitimate to others, they will attribute it to you.

This means that the real-world definitions exist in the mental realities created and maintained by those you talk to and listen to—your circle or the relationships and cultures you are embedded in. You can't "have" something that is not justified in the eyes of others. You *can* have what you can successfully express.

People experience pain and pleasure differently. But what you can have when any other people are concerned depends upon how you perform that pain or that pleasure. And in any culture where pain gives you more status than does pleasure, you are more likely to have pains rather than pleasures—in modern Western cultures specifically.

Pleasure is harder to talk about than pain (in our culture). We assume that pain is inflicted on you. We assume that pleasure is something you have to achieve. Most people are vaguely dissatisfied with their lives. That's because those are the kinds of feelings that are expected. To speak of your pleasures seems to be boasting. So instead of boasting about our health, we boast about our illnesses.

None of this should be taken to suggest that we do not have subjective experiences of likes and dislikes—of all sorts. There is an anonymous English jingle that captures this:

"There was a faith-healer of Deal
Who said, 'Although pain isn't real,
If I sit on a pin
And it punctures my skin,
I dislike what I fancy I feel.'"

Our experiences are all privately our own. They are subjective. To speak of them or to express them in any other way requires we do so by attempting to make them objective—that is, acknowledged by the others we want to acknowledge them. Then we are stuck with the legitimacy of having them. We are stuck with how they get interpreted in the world outside of us.

It isn't that we don't subjectively experience them. It is that for them to be "real"—even for you—they must be legitimated by others in how they talk about them.

One further caveat for doing life as you would have it done:

It has long been observed that when pleasure becomes
the business of life, it ceases to be pleasure.

When pain is the business of life, it becomes banal. It ceases to be of interest to others. Beyond what's justified in the eyes of others, it becomes simply boring.

For those who would do life as they would have it done, keep in mind that people are *explainers,* and that our explanations widely shared become our reality. You can explain anything, if others will "buy" your explanation. It's *how* you explain things by your prowess in performing them in the presence of others that matters.

XVI

. . . Your Habitat:
Inner and Outer

"Is there no way out of the mind?"

—Sylvia Plath, 1971

*"The mind is hindered by too little
education—and by too much."*

—Blaise Pascal

Our resourceful satirist Evan Esar offered this observation in one of his columns:

"There are two kinds of fools: mindful and mindless."

In this he was echoing the 17th-century French mathematician, physicist, and theologian Blaise Pascal (above). How can one's mind be hindered by too little education—or by too much? How can the mindful and the mindless both be "fools" of the one kind or the other?

One thing is certain—no equivocation. It is that your mind mediates everything. Your mind processes everything that goes on in you or around you. It processes what you think, what you feel, and what you do. It produces the meaning of everything you attend to—inner or outer.

It is the source of everything you believe about who you were, who you are, and who you will be. It is what you are capable of and what you are not capable of. It is not just a handy tool. It is the master and you are its slave.

What you can't conceive of, you won't conceive of. What you can't imagine you won't imagine. What you can't speak of, you won't speak of.

What you know of the world around you is both enabled and constrained by your mind.

You can't go anywhere or do anything without it. So the answer to Sylvia Plath's question above—*Is there no way out of the mind?*—is plainly and simply, No. Your mind archives what you believe, what you know, what you have or could imagine, what you feel about things, and what you can or cannot do about anything you can think of.

It is your constant companion. You can talk to it according to how you are capable, and it can talk back to you according to how *it* is capable. It is subject to flights of fancy. It is subject to the yoke of rationality, as Pascal observed. It is not your servant. It is your master. The English poet Sir Edward Dyer penned, *"My mind to me a kingdom is / Such perfect joy therein I find / That it excels all other bliss . . . ."*

At any given moment, there is nothing you can do beyond going along for the ride, however distasteful or foolish or wrongheaded it may be. It will take you where it is built to go. It may be, at any given moment, incapable of taking you where you might want to go. You don't control it. It controls you. It is your refuge from a world you cannot conquer.

Within the limits of where you have to start from, you do have the long range advantage. You can remodel it, redesign it, refurnish it, or improve upon its routines. This is Archimedes' fulcrum. Given a place to stand, you can move your mind out of its ruts and into other worlds where it is still the master—but where you are its architect.

In his *Phrases and Philosophies for the Use of the Young,* the playful mind of Oscar Wilde suggested:

"Only the shallow know themselves."

This is not true, of course. But it is a provocative metaphor for those who intend to do life as they would have it done. The metaphor might lead us to this insight: The wider and the deeper runs your mind, the more likely it is that you can call upon the resources you need for doing life. Others you know may not appreciate this. This may be why so many people are "shallow." They cling to familiarity and changelessness.

To do life as you would have it done requires you to break out of your ruts, your habits, and replace them with the kinds of habits that can serve your purposes. There is little security in changing yourself. That's why most people don't—until eventually they no longer can.

Back in 1968, the philosopher Alan Watts published a book entitled *The Wisdom of Insecurity*. We dealt with this at some length in Chapter V. Here we just need to remind ourselves that doing life as you would have it done involves risking your security. If you intend not to be who others believe you to be, you have to disrupt the security of their certainties if you are going to forge new relationships with them or others.

You can't become someone else by clinging to who you are.

Your Interior Habitat

Your primary habitat is your own mind. Your mind is the medium though which everything you take into account—whether about you or anything in the rest of the world—gets translated, interpreted. Your mind is the repository of all of the meanings you normally assign to yourself, to others, or to what is going on inside or outside of you.

What you know or believe about yourself or the rest of the world—what things *mean* to you—is a function of your own mind. It is your primary habitat—the place where you live your life.

The healthier it is, the healthier you will be. The richer it is in meanings, the richer you will be in the meaning of your life. The better it functions, the better you will function.

When you have no guiding purpose in life, your mind will be a hodge-podge. It will consist of whatever comes your way. You will be who people want you to be. The outside world of people and things will clone you. You will be a product of whatever external forces chance upon you.

It is only when you have a guiding purpose in life that you have need of a mind that serves to further your interests. Otherwise it will serve its own interests.

Doing life as you would have it done is just such a guiding purpose. It requires you to have the kind of mind that puts you on the right path and keeps you on the path you need to be on. An undisciplined mind cannot do this.

The influential French author Andre Gide wrote in his preface to Antoine de Saint-Exupery's *Night Flight* (1931) about Saint-Exupery's paradoxical truth:

> " . . . *which seems to me of great psychological import: that man's happiness lies not in freedom but in his acceptance of a duty."*

Culturally, we have taken the path of freedom rather than duty. That may be why "happiness" for us has become so elusive.

To set forth on the path of doing life as you would have it done requires you to see your purpose in life not so much as a choice, but as a duty—to yourself. It becomes a duty that can only be fulfilled by composing your mind to provide the discipline you need to fulfill that duty.

If you don't have the kind of internal habitat you need to do life as you would have it done, you won't be able to do life in that way.

The foundation of that internal habitat is your duty to yourself to fulfill your purpose in life. All the rest is built on that foundation. Without it, your habitat will have no integrity. It will be whimsical. The only people who have "character" are those who are engaged in fulfilling their duty . . . to themselves.

And this can be pursued only in the world in which you live—your external habitat. You cannot enter that world except through the mediation of your own mind. The world you perceive tells you more about who you are than about what that outer world seems to be.

Saint-Exupery also believed that our only way of escaping the debilitating impermanence of our own lives . . .

> ". . . is through self-dedication and a focusing of the mind not on things-in-themselves, but on that which gives them meaning . . . ,"

as the translator of Exupery's *The Wisdom of the Sands*, Stuart Gilbert, put it. You have no way of getting directly to "things-in-themselves." You can grasp them only by your own mind. Your mind does not—cannot—deal with "things-in-themselves," but only with what they mean to you.

What makes the world meaningful—and you in it—are the minds that make that world meaningful. Your mind is the source of what gives things their meaning. In that sense, life is always a self-fulfilling prophecy. *As things mean to you, so will they be.*

The mind is your interior habitat. That dwelling produces your being, all of the conditions of your life. Who you are is first a matter of what you mean to yourself. That is what you carry into all the rest of the world.

Your External Habitat

Many of the dilemmas and problems of life come from confusing the inner and the outer.

The dictum for which the French philosopher and mathematician Rene Descartes is best known is—

> "'*Cogito, ergo sum*': I think, therefore I am."

It is not enough, and Descartes knew that it was not. He had his own way of unpacking what seems to be so profound that philosophers have for years been discussing their interpretations of his pithy saying.

It is not enough because it does not tell us *how* to think in order to be who we will thus *become*. Thinking has consequences—good *and* bad. It is the good consequences you want. How should you think in order to become who you intend to become?

The famous Scottish philosopher David Hume wrote (in 1757):

> *"Beauty is no quality in things themselves. It exists merely in the mind which contemplates them."*

This is useful to you in a number of ways:

- There is no justice—or any other human quality—in things themselves. The qualities you attribute to others or to the world exist solely in your mind.

- The fact that others around you agree doesn't put those qualities in the things themselves. It merely means you share similar qualities of mind.

- When you make a judgment about anything, you must recognize thoroughly that it is your mind that is making the judgment. No matter that others agree with you. They may be the source of your judgment—or at least the vindication of it.

- It is an easy mistake to make because your mind is also your habitat, but you are likely to assume that what is going on in your head is "reality." The way in which you contemplate things is always and inescapably the way your mind works.

- The way your mind works is not necessarily the way the world works. It is also not the way others' minds work.

- A great many human and social problems arise from the failure to keep these conditions in mind. They arise from the attempted imposition of one mind (or one set of minds) on another.

You must see that there is an outer world that you inhabit. You must come to terms with this fact: that world is in no way obligated to be as you think it is or say it is.

Your outer habitat—that world outside of you—consists of two autonomous parts:

One is the social world of people and their doings, and the artifacts of their doings—what the people before you and around you believe, and what they have made out of their beliefs and their imaginations. Things like the telephone and the idea of "freedom" are such human artifacts. We will come to grips with the second part of that world a bit later.

Most critters are hard-wired to be as they are and do as they do. We humans are almost infinitely plastic. We *invent* our ways of being—for better or for worse. We invent that social and physical habitat, and then it invents us, as Churchill said about our buildings.

We have no collective destiny except the one that has been invented for us by those who preceded us, or by those who presently most influence us.

No one, including you, can have a conscious life apart from that outer social habitat. You have to be *someone* to other people. And the only way to do that is by becoming one of them—joining in the social milieu being continuously adhered to and yet continuously being remodeled by you and by billions of other people doing "their thing."

Most of those other people in this non-tribal, "modern" world you inhabit are people you do not and cannot know. Yet they anonymously affect your life in myriad ways. A bunch of people you do not know determine what you consume on television, including the commercials. A bunch of people you do not know make the laws and regulations that impact you. No one controls the stock market because "everyone" does.

Our modern habitat is awash with influences both seen and unseen. We drive cars we couldn't build along highways and streets that we didn't put there. We don't go where we go. We go where *they* go.

You don't know what the agendas are of all of those anonymous people who impact the conditions of your life. If you fall in line, you go where they and their artifacts take you. If you become a victim of their agendas through the use of their ideas and their computers (for example), you become one of the millions of clichés required to support them.

We become addicted to whatever tools and toys we employ to navigate our lives. If they "belong" to us, we belong to them.

In 1847, the indispensable American philosopher and poet Ralph Waldo Emerson wrote:

> *"Things are in the saddle,*
> *And ride mankind."*

That was more than a century and a half ago. Since then, the "things" we buy and use have become exponentially more "in the saddle." We are being ridden by those things far more today than in 1847.

Those things may be tangible, like cars and planes and high-rise buildings and computers and highways and cell phones. But they are also intangible—like ideas, concepts, beliefs, feelings. We are like waves breaking unpredictably on the shore. The "shore," as communication theorist Joshua Meyrowitz put it in his book *No Sense of Place*, is no longer a place. More and more of us live in cyberspace, which is everywhere yet nowhere.

Meyrowitz's 1985 book was about the electronic media. But it applies to other technologies that we use every day. Our restlessness and need to be in constant motion but constant contact has enabled us to have no "place" where vital events with others can actually take place. So we have lost sight of where it was we wanted to go.

William Morris was a famous English writer, artist, and designer (among other accomplishments). He was the author of *News from Nowhere (1891)*, a socialist, utopian work. It was popular in his time. Other than serving as a precursor to our present-day malaise, his title predicted the anonymity that has clouded our sense of direction.

In his *Hopes and Fears for Art (1882),* he wrote (and Steve Jobs may have taken his caveat to heart):

> *"Have nothing in your houses that you do not know*
> *to be useful, or believe to be beautiful."*

If we here substitute *minds* (our inescapable habitat) for *houses*, we would have the formula for a right life:

> *Have nothing in your minds that you do not know*
> *to be useful, or believe to be beautiful.*

We would only need to add a definition for "useful"—in this case useful to your good and worthy purposes in life. There is much we make use of in our lives that could not meet this criterion. People who do not have good and worthy purposes in life make things "useful" for lesser reasons. We do not follow those who can furnish our minds with what we believe to be beautiful. We follow our celebrities and our consumer materialism. Both demean you.

Still, our most intractable problems come from our failure to distinguish the realities of our inner habitat (our minds) from the realities of our outer habitat—the residue of what millions of people before us have thought and believed and thus stuffed our culture with.

The lessons bear repeating:

> *Do not mistake what is going on in your mind for what*
> *is going on in others' minds. Do not mistake your*
> *interpretations for what is going on in the world. Do not*
> *mistake what is said about what is going on in the*
> *world for what is actually going on in the world. Stick*
> *with the boundaries. These are two different worlds.*

There was a Canadian sociologist (Orrin Klapp) who had a clever way of helping us remember how important it is to adhere to the boundary between the two:

> *"There is WIGO—what is going on. And then there is*
> *WIMTH—what it means to humans."*

We have to live in the world of WIGO. But the only way we have of doing so is by consulting WIMTH. They are two different worlds. The only way we have of grasping WIGO is via our human explanations of it—WIMTH.

Particularly, what it means to *you* personally (which is inevitably a byproduct of WIMTH in general).

When you mistake what something means to you for what is going on in the world, you create problems for yourself. You also create problems in that other world of WIGO. For your own health and welfare, you need to keep these worlds clearly separated at all times. You need to do this as well for the health and welfare of all of those around you and for all the rest of the world of people and their artifacts (for politicians as well as your family doctor), as Confucius taught more than seven centuries ago.

Human Nature

There is no universal "human nature" beyond the human proclivity for learning some language, and to use that language to explain ourselves to ourselves and to explain to each other whatever seems relevant about our lives in the rest of the world.

And this always occurs in *some* culture—some civilization (e.g., the Maya, the aboriginal Australians) some society of humans. There is no evidence of a human in human history except in some human/social context.

People talk to and with each other, in some language, in some cultural context. In doing so, they create their inner habitat—their minds. And then they create all manner of sacred and utilitarian artifacts to facilitate their lives in the worlds they have thus created. There have always been wars. There have always been illnesses. There have always been rites of passage from birth to death.

These have been differently explained and differently dealt with in different human cultures. There was no Wall Street until money became our own peculiar way of ordering society. Our Western Bible says that "In the beginning was the Word . . . ." We create ourselves and our worlds as we go along. In this, our minds play the pivotal role.

The "collective mind" constitutes the source of our outer human/social habitat. We have to live with that. No one of us controls that. In that sense it seems "natural"—out of our control. It is constantly being percolated by every one of us. The product is our mental habitat—the world as we know it, and yourself as you know yourself.

We are perhaps the most plastic of all animals on earth. We are therefore the most adaptable. "People" can adapt to almost any physical environment, almost any political environment, almost any way of being and doing. This doesn't make us superior. It only makes us the most adaptable.

The English Field Marshall Lord Raglan (1788-1855) said:

> *"Culture is roughly anything we do and the monkeys don't."*

We live in and by some human culture or other. It is what gives us the claim to be human. Some people created it. Others remodeled it and still do. Still others maligned it. We talk. In our talk we create things. In our talk we live in our culture in order to change it. Like plate tectonics, that change occurs very slowly and unseen. Those who come after us will usually adapt to it. Otherwise, the collective will cease to exist.

By adapting, you can only have the life you already have. This would be a good place to revisit our Irish philosopher and playwright George Bernard Shaw, who so eloquently revealed the price of adaptation. The critical struggle in doing life as you would have it done is always that between status quo and change. Here's the way Shaw put it:

> *"The reasonable [person] adapts . . . to the world. The*
> *unreasonable one persists in trying to adapt the world*
> *to himself. Therefore all progress depends on the*
> *unreasonable [person]."*

To do life as you would have it done requires you to *persist* in trying to get the world to adapt to you. It requires you to be (in this sense) unreasonable.

You can't change in the direction you want unless you unreasonably refuse to adapt to the circumstances you already have. You have to change those circumstances. If you change your habitat, you change yourself.

You are likely familiar with Reinhold Niebuhr's "Serenity Prayer":

> *"God grant me the serenity*
> *to accept things I cannot change;*
> *courage to change the things I can;*
> *and wisdom to know the difference."*

People agonize more about the things they cannot change than about the things they can. You can change yourself. But you can't really change the world to suit you. To change yourself, you need not just courage. You need the competencies required to do so. Along the lines of Gandhi's recipe for changing the world—"If you want to change the world, change yourself"—where is a person who can't change herself to get wisdom?

In this prayer, accept that you are the only god who can grant what is asked for.

The "Natural" World

The other part of your outer habitat is, of course, the "natural" world. Physiologically and biologically, you are composed of "natural" components. Your body was and is a natural thing. It has its own logic which is what makes it a part of your natural habitat.

You may be conscious of your body. You may be able to name its components (according to the current man-made knowledge about it). You may be able to describe how it feels, using the man-made concepts you have available to you.

You may also be more or less conscious of the larger natural world you inhabit—the trees, the sky, the water, the land. As our tools got more powerful, we altered our natural habitat. We have fouled our own nest. Instead of collaborating with our natural habitat, we continue to "conquer" it.

This habitat must be sacred to make our inner and outer habitats sacred. If they are not, they are merely disposable. Unless you want to be disposable yourself, you will find a way to make your habitats sacred—that is, to be the way they need to be for your life and your destiny.

The natural world cares not for your desires. If we do not care for it, it will not care for us. If we do not care for our families, they will not care for us. If we do not care for our institutions, they will not care for us.

We despoil people in the same way we despoil our natural habitat. We despoil our cultures in the same way we despoil our natural habitats. We interpret them to suit our petty interests of the moment.

Wisdom runs deeper than that. If you intend to do life as it should be done for your own best interests, you first have to create the habitat(s) in which that is possible. And then enrich it with all your might.

Pain and Pleasure

Pain and pleasure are examples of what you experience in your inner habitat. They, like all inner feeling, are absolutely private. No one else has access to your inner experiences.

Yet, if you want your experience to have some reality to other people—thus legitimating your inner feeling—you have to be able to express it in ways others will "understand." Here we can readily see the interdependent nature of the inner feelings and their legitimacy in the social world. If you want your experiences to seem real to you because they are "witnessed" by others, you have to communicate them so that they will be witnessed by others as you express or perform them.

Anyone can say, "I love you." It is only when another person pretends to understand what you meant by what you said that it becomes real to you. Anyone can say, "I am in pain." It is only when another person acknowledges what you said that it now exists in the external, "real," world.

The lessons here are perverse but incontrovertible:

- It is very unlikely that you will have a feeling which is not already legitimated in your culture. Unless you invent it and it gets added to the culturally-approved list for expressing and thus for "having." Romantic love is not a universal sentiment.

- It is only the feelings that you can acceptably audition before others that you can legitimately "have."

- What you *can* experience is culturally derived. *You* might believe it, but most cultures would not permit you to play the role of God.

- What you cannot express satisfactorily you cannot "have." What you do express satisfactorily you are justified in "having."

- The feelings you *can* have are those you are permitted by others to "have."

Our cultural bias in the direction of individual autonomy and self-justification has made these conditions of our inner feelings—pain or pleasure or hundreds of others—all but invisible to us, even irrelevant.

They are not. They are at the same time the pitfalls of doing life, and the price of doing life as you would have it done. It's relatively easy to have the kinds of feelings that are socially-sanctioned. As the social satirist Evan Esar said,

> "Petting is popular everywhere probably because it creates a lot of good feeling."

And also because it is, in some form, socially sanctioned.

It is difficult to express the feelings you need to do life as you would choose if they are not socially-sanctioned. As the famous French author Balzac (1799-1850) quipped:

> "Life is simply what our feelings do to us."

This means you've got to have the right ones. Yet the right ones are not guaranteed in any culture.

You can't have an inner habitat without the existence of an outer habitat (the social, the cultural, the physical). That outer habitat makes you who you are. It both constrains and enables. But neither the constraints nor the possibilities will take you—or your social world—in the direction of your intended destiny.

There is always a price to be paid for doing life as you would have it done. If life is what our feelings do to us, the feelings *necessary* for doing life as you would have it done will be fraught with obstacles to be overcome. The fabric of your life is something you have to weave with great care and diligence. It is woven of your feelings about things.

XVII

. . . Illusions and Delusions

"Truths are illusions of which one has forgotten that they are illusions."

—*Nietzsche*

"Reality is a shared hallucination."

—*Howard Bloom*

It is a tough thing for rational people to come to grips with the fact that we live in and by our illusions—our myths and our explanations.

Our minds—our inner habitats—consist of beliefs and perceptions that have been created by all of those people who came before us, and all of the people who surround us. We inhabit the illusions that we and others have created in talking about them the way we do.

Our culturally-determined concepts of beauty and truth are but base examples of how humans have created the worlds they inhabit in their minds by how they have talked about them. Our brains exist in the tangible world. Our minds do not.

Even so, our brains *are* what we say they are—how we have defined them in the past and now in the present. Whatever they were in wordless times, they served us more or less well.

Minds are created in communication. They are maintained or altered in communication. They exist in mental space. They can be affected by damage to the brain or even to a leg. We have that sense of our bodies and its parts that arises in how we talk about them.

What we perceive is now a function of our minds because we create everything we know by the way we talk about it. To call what you or I know an illusion is simply to say that the way we see the world was created by what our predecessors said about it. And by what our contemporaries say about it. And by what *you* or I say about it.

This is not easy to chew on and digest. But it is a far more pragmatic place to stand than to presume that what you grasp with words is *reality.* Our words transform things from what they "are" to how we understand them. We perceive ourselves and our worlds essentially by how we talk about them.

The Polish writer Stanislaw J. Lec warned us:

> *"Everything is an illusion, including this notion."*

This gets at the challenge you face. You can't avoid illusion by the pursuit of "truth." If Lec's pronouncement is useful, then all "truths," no matter how useful they may be, are themselves illusions. As he says, *everything*—even his own observation—is an illusion. You can only create (for your purposes) more useful illusions.

This was in part the counter-intuitive appeal of the first novel: Cervantes' *Don Quixote* (1605-15). In it, Quixote is given to express one of the major themes of the story:

> *"Too much sanity may be madness. And the maddest of all, to see life as it is and not as it should be!"*

If you seek to do life as you would have it done, this spells out certain imperatives of your perspectives on life:

- We live in a civilization that musters its "science" and its related forces to determine life as it is, not as it should be. This is the first obstacle you will encounter.

- And a huge obstacle it may be. People will be eager to help you "find" yourself. But they typically want no part of any attempts you might make to remodel yourself in a chosen direction. That's because their continuity depends on your staying as you are.

LEE THAYER

- "Too much sanity" may translate as too much rationality. We want to understand things by taking them apart. Quixote's philosophy? Your aim should not be understanding as such, but life itself. You may understand. But you DO life. Should you do life as it is, or as it should be?

- Should you accept life as it is, or strive ever to make life as it should be? Our culture encourages the "as it is" part, and we are nudged into the position of seeing life as it is—not life as it *should* be. Since both are illusions, we confuse the one with the other.

- It is far, far easier to adapt to the conditions of your life as they are than it is to undertake changing those conditions in the direction of what they *should* be. Our illusion, guaranteed by the commercial media, is that the easier path is the right path.

- You can't *buy* the right life. But you can buy the things that make your life as it is more tolerable.

- Besides, you are surrounded by people who want you to be as you are, not as you "should" be.

Quixote's illusions were closer to the actualities he faced than were those that had become customary in his day. For example, he says:

> "I have always heard, Sancho [his companion], that doing
> good to base fellows is like throwing water into the sea."

If you want good done to you by those who are capable, you must do what is necessary to avoid being "base"—that is, commonplace, less than worthy, ignorant and proud of it.

You ultimately cannot do good for yourself without the support of others. Then it is a matter of *which* others. Not just any others will do. You have to surround yourself—literally or virtually—by those whose minds will support the one *you* need to do life as you would have it done.

The tragedy of Don Quixote was that he could not find like-minded people (those who see life not as it is but as it should be). So he got much abuse from the base fellows (and women) he encountered. They didn't understand him because they couldn't.

You're up against the same indifference to your aspirations.

Our greatest illusions are those we hold about ourselves. The Swiss writer and philosopher Henri Amiel set forth in his journal of 1853:

> *"Our greatest illusion is to believe that we are what we think ourselves to be."*

You can take this in two ways. One is that the "we" here is most people in our civilization—our culture. But the more useful way is individual. Your illusion is to believe that what you *are* is what you think yourself to be.

What you think yourself to be emerges from what you say you are to yourself. And that is always produced and prompted by what other people think you are.

Do not take such illusions lightly. They constitute the only reality you will ever have. The advantage is that if you are determined to change yourself, it is your and others' illusions about who you are that need changing. The "reality" you have to change is itself illusory.

You have to change yourself by changing the way you interpret yourself in the world. You have to change others' illusions about you in the most tangible ways. They experience you. Change the way they experience you. You experience yourself. Change the way you do so.

They will remain illusions. But they could be the kinds of illusions that serve your purposes in doing life as you would have it done. They may be illusions. But they bear as reality on the changes you may need to make.

The American psychiatrist Alan Watts was fond of saying:

> *"A thing is a think."*

It is how you think about things that determines how you see those things. This is as much the case for the events of your life as it is for the people and the things and the ideas that you make a part of your life. It is not what they *are*. It is how you think about them.

You have radically different *feelings* about the people and the things you love than you do about the people or the things toward which you are indifferent. The opposite of love is not hate but indifference. When you commit to someone or something, you are then supposed to be indifferent to others or to other ways of life.

What this implies is that you need to love the people and the ideas and the things that will enable you to do life as you would have it done. And you have to be more or less indifferent to those that would take you off course.

If you think you cannot do this, then you cannot do life as you would have it done. It may be made to seem predestined—that you would fall in love with this person and ignore another who might be better for you. You may like to think you do not *choose* what you love and what you are indifferent to. But you have to understand those as your *choice*.

If you are a victim of life—of being done to rather than doing life—then you will suffer the victim's fate. In our culture, we live under the cloud of victimization. We have made it pay to be a victim of life rather than a maker of life.

If you buy into *this* illusion, you will be lost to yourself. You will be a victim of the vagaries of life rather than the "captain" of your own ship, your own life.

Is what you "want" real or is it an illusion? The German-born psychoanalyst and social philosopher Erich Fromm prompted us to think of it this way:

> *"Modern man lives under the illusion that he knows what*
> *he wants, while he actually wants what he is* supposed
> *to want."*

You may think you know what you want. But you have to separate that from the influences on you that make you want what you are *supposed* to want. There is a big difference. The influences on you from your outer habitat (especially the commercial media and your close friends and confidantes) are more likely to lead you in the direction of what you are supposed to want.

At the same time, the illusion you could be living under is that you know what you want—for all good reasons.

To be disillusioned is always embarrassing, if not painful. We may do without our daily bread, but we cannot do without our daily illusion, as one pre-Nazi German political leader (Gustav Stresemann) put it. Our illusions are indispensable to us.

Gustave Le Bon, the 19th-20th century French sociologist who was noted for his "crowd psychology," once remarked:

> *"Many men easily do without truth but none is strong enough to do without illusions."*

The arguments about "truth" over the millennia have been mostly about the methods of arriving at what was referred to as "the truth." In our time, the truth is what is arrived at by experiment or by research. We believe now in "science." At one time we believed in our spiritual sources to tell us what was true. Before that, we believed in the folklore of the day.

What you need to know is that truths are as much illusions as illusions are our truths.

The early 20th-century child star Shirley Temple was quoted as saying:

> *"I stopped believing in Santa Claus when I was six. Mother took me to see him in a department store, and he asked for my autograph."*

One way of interpreting this is that she stopped believing in Santa Claus (or said so) and substituted believing in her stardom, which was prompted by the department store Santa Claus's request. Santa Claus is "real" to those who believe in him. He is not real to those who do not. It is not only beauty but truth that is in the eye of the beholder. It is a condition of being human.

This brings us around to the lesson for those who would like to do life rather than be done to by it. Our satirical columnist Evan Esar offered this observation:

"Self-deception is the illusion of the person who believes
that he has no illusions."

Accept your truths (or beliefs) as illusions. Seek to supply yourself with the illusions (your personal beliefs or truths) that will get you where you want to go. Do not import those that are merely the fashions of the day.

Illusions may be thought of as those personal and private beliefs that constitute your "truths." The question is not the academic one of what is "true." It is the *pragmatic* one of where your socially-derived or socially-concocted beliefs are going to lead you.

They could be right. They could be wrong. It all depends upon the consequences of believing this or that. Your illusions (or truths—they are interchangeable here) about yourself or the world outside of you are those that will bear upon the life you have, and the life you might have.

Delusions are widely-held illusions on the part of the cultures or the societies to which you belong. In the same way that your personal illusions can lead you astray, the delusions of a whole society can lead it astray. Examples would be the Roman Empire, the Aztec, the Anasazi, and dozens of other extinct civilizations. They had popular beliefs that led to their failure.

This phenomenon is dealt with comprehensively in the article by the UCLA professor Jared Diamond, "Why Do Some Societies Make Disastrous Decisions?" (in the John Brockman-edited collection entitled *Culture*). In it Diamond sets forth "a roadmap of factors in failures of group decision-making." He writes:

> *"Perhaps if we understand the reasons why groups make*
> *bad decisions, we can use that knowledge as a checklist*
> *to help groups make good decisions."*

The lesson here for doing life as you would have it done is that there is as much waywardness in the decision-making of groups and societies as there is in your private illusions. If you buy into the often tacit beliefs of the collectives to which you belong, you could be along for the ride to extinction.

Or to hell, as an attributed Buddhist saying sets it forth:

"Delusion injures others, bring hardships to oneself, soils the mind, and may well lead to hell."

But what is a person like you to do? There are only two options:

- To share what others in your collective believe, or

- To believe in your own illusions.

Either way, you are risking. If you follow your own (your own "drummer"), you will be dismissed or even excommunicated by the true believers in your collective. If you follow the beliefs of the collective, you put yourself at risk of the fate of the collective.

The poet Schiller once said,

"Anyone taken as an individual is tolerably sensible and reasonable—as a member of a crowd he at once becomes a blockhead."

This is taken from the collection *Extraordinary Popular Delusions and the Madness of Crowds,* by Charles Mackey, LL.D., first published in 1841.

We see this crowd psychology at work even today. People are often fairly reasonable until they get into a crowd. Then, with their adrenaline flowing, they behave as if they were mad. Collectives offer people that opportunity: to behave badly. We see it at contested soccer matches. Is it possible that the fans of the most popular television programs are also victims of a "crowd psychology"?

The decisions that are taken by a crowd—even a crowd of people desperately seeking relevance—often appear to be irrational. Why they do what they do seems just to happen. Decisions and actions are frequently not traceable to any one source.

Helpful to those who would do life as they would have it done is this quip by Lily Tomlin:

> *"After all, what is reality anyway? Nothin' but a*
> *collective hunch."*

You don't have to be a Lily Tomlin fan to appreciate that. The book Jane Wagner wrote for Lily Tomlin's one-person show, *The Search for Signs of Intelligent Life in the Universe,* was subsequently made into a movie. Our collective hunches are the basis for the book by ex-longshoreman Eric Hoffer: *The True Believer.* What Wagner and Tomlin made humorous, Hoffer made serious.

A person who is seriously trying to do life as it should be done will be suspected of some form of insanity. None of the "sane" people are trying to do this. You may have a problem with these suspicions. In the same stage play, Lily Tomlin's character is given to say:

> *"You're thinkin': How does a person know if they're crazy*
> *or not? Well, sometimes you don't know. Sometimes you*
> *can go through life suspecting you are*
> *but never really knowing for sure. Sometimes you know for sure*
> *'cause you've got so many people tellin' you you're crazy*
> *that it's your word against everyone else's."*

To undertake doing life as you would have it done puts you outside the cultural norms. It makes you wrong in the eyes of those who believe they are right simply because they've got the numbers on their side. So don't talk about it. Just do it.

The Hungarian-born American psychiatrist and iconoclast Thomas Szasz defined delusion in the following way:

> *"Delusion: belief said to be false by someone who doesn't*
> *share it."*

You can do something with this. The people who don't share your desire for doing life as you would have it done will call your commitment a delusion. It may be. But keep in mind: so also may their way of doing life be a delusion. It all depends not on the delusions by which you live, but where they are taking you.

Theirs is an adaptation to most others, wherever most others may be destined. It's easier just to go along with the crowd. The humanist writer and naturalist Annie Dillard once wrote (in "This *Is* the Life"):

> *"Any culture tells you how to live your one and only*
> *life: to wit, as everyone else does."*

If you don't live your one and only life as everyone else does, you will be subject to sanctions, if not treatment. Those who are locked up in loony bins may be crazy. So may be their inquisitors. Some get locked up because they are not thinking and acting like everyone else does.

And fashions in comportment come and go, like every other fashion. If you are serious about doing life as you would have it done, you may have to comport yourself in at least partial seclusion. This is what artists have had to do. Sometimes they create a club of like-minded people having its own culture—do's and don'ts about how to think, what to believe, how to feel about what, where to go, etc.

The gay "community" has its places and secret codes and mannerisms just like every other community. There's a reason why criminals prefer the company of other criminals. There's a reason why true believers of any stripe prefer true believers of the same stripe.

This raises a cultural dilemma which has been argued from the earliest days to the present day. It has been exacerbated in our epoch by two legacies:

- One is the legacy of scientism in our day. That's the belief (or delusion, if you will) that "science" will eventually give us the ultimate answers to everything. It races along in the name of rationality, seeking to answer every non-rational phenomenon which people would like to understand—or control, including the stock market and other people.

- The other is the legacy of evolutionism, which started far before Darwin. That carries with it (for pseudo-scientists) the *a priori* endorsement that whoever we are and whatever we do is more or less predetermined by our genes or something else biological. This may be, of course. But it is only one kind of explanation. It happens to be the most culturally-accepted one in our day. But just because it underlies so much of our thinking these days does not make it true. It is simply the hegemonic worldview.

For those who would like to learn how to do life as they would have it done, this raises a significant dilemma. Are you determined by your biological inheritance? Or are you free to choose your course?

There are pseudo-scientists in every direction you look. They can tell you why you are the way you are, and why you do what you do. Even the mind is being reduced to the neurology of the brain, in spite of the caveat of the Canadian brain surgeon who at the time had been in more brain pans than anyone else. He concluded: *"I can't tell you where the mind is. But I can tell you it is not in the brain."*

Popular delusions are always more powerful than any evidence to the contrary.

Biological reductionism is rampant. But here's the rub: So far as is known, there has never been research on a single animal who had not been exposed to others of its kind. All have lived in social environments. It's difficult (impossible?) to believe that some humans were born with a gene that pre-determined their participation in demonstrations, for example It is also difficult to believe that humans (for whom "love" is the most discussed subject)—have intercourse because they want their sperm and eggs to be the ones to survive. They seem to be using other criteria.

You weren't born knowing who to be in the human world. Or what to do, or wear, or say, or feel. You had to learn these things. Unless the ultimate research is conducted, it is impossible to separate the contribution of one's nature from one's nurture. But given that we can uniquely invent ourselves by how we explain ourselves, bet on nurture.

You live in a social world, only minimally in a "natural" one. So do evolutionists. They do not personally comport themselves much different from other people. They either suffer the same bad genes. Or just maybe the same delusions.

Even if you are wrong, bet on social determinacy. It is the only way you can have a place to stand to try doing life as you would have it done. Can you imagine that Gandhi was or that Charles Manson was genetically predetermined to do what they did? How about Horowitz? Was he genetically predetermined to be a great concert pianist? Or Picasso to change his painting style as he did?

Or you to contemplate doing life as it should be done?

The great *biologist* D'Arcy Thomson once said:

> "*Things are the way they are because they got to*
> *be that way.*"

Was he predestined to say that? Or was it a conviction of his from his years of study that he wanted to share with the rest of us?

Things are the way they are in your life because they got to be that way. If they somehow got to be that way, they could somehow be some other way. That may be the delusion you need to go by.

The Dutch humanist and scholar Erasmus, who lived in the late 15th and early 16th centuries, made this observation in his book *The Praise of Folly*:

> "*The more ways a man is deluded, the happier he is.*"

It's unlikely that most pseudo-scientists would endorse that. But then we see very few of them who seem to be happy.

Ambrose Bierce (the author of *The Devil's Dictionary*) despised realism, which he defined as "The art of depicting nature as it is seen by toads." What he offered us about delusions was this:

> *"All are lunatics, but he who can analyze his delusions*
> *is called a philosopher."*

Assuming you want to do life pragmatically and not philosophically, you don't want to analyze your delusions. You want to choose those that suit your purposes.

XVIII

. . . Relevance and Irrelevance

"Any idiot can face a crisis. It's this day-to-day living that wears you out."

—Anton Chekhov

"Individuals are often the last to hear what it concerns themselves the most to know."

—Thomas Paine

The perpetual problem of life is "Who am I?" If not that, then "Who should I aspire to be?" And, if not that, "What should I do with my life?"

These are big questions. Most people are caught up in the trivia of everyday living, as Chekhov suggested. They may not spend much time thinking about these big questions. But the decisions and choices they make in their day-to-day living channel their present and future lives. In that sense, the big questions get answered by the small choices that we make every minute of our waking hours.

They do get answered. Life goes on. But they get answered indirectly, by how we perform our lives in our day-to-day living.

Should you care? Most people do the life they were handed. All people "have" a life. It might not be the one they would choose in their fantasy moments about it. There are three reasons for simply living out the life you were handed:

- You don't care enough one way or another about the life you happen to "have." You may complain. But that will be to other people who have also settled for whatever comes their way.

- Or, you can't imagine what an alternative might actually be like.

- Or, you believe you haven't got what it would take to change yourself inside-out.

The longer you live, the harder it is to make course corrections. Your habits (well-worn ruts) constitute a status quo. Your day-to-day ossifies. It is far, far easier to continue as you are than to make any significant changes—no matter how much you might dream of doing so.

In the seemingly endless struggle between life as it is and life as you would have it be, life as it is will almost always win. Ingrained habits and routines are far more powerful than mere wishes or dreams.

You have to kill your status quo in order to escape it. There is no passion in the status quo. There is only grinding on. But your status quo is a bundle of habits and routines developed over many years. They are who you are. If you would be someone else, you have to kill who you are. Otherwise you are stuck with the life you have. You may do so little by little. But the life you are regularly perform is familiar and predictable.

There can be no significant change in who you are as long as you are a victim of who you are.

Relevance is always a major factor. It helps to look at this in two directions:

- What or whom is relevant to you? And conversely,

- To what or to whom are you relevant?

This comes down to a matter of what has mindshare for you, and in what ways you are a part of others' mindshare. Love is mutual mindshare (or heart-share—it is ultimately the same thing). When you think about someone all the time obsessively, that's love. When you both do, you are eager to consummate your relationship, because you imagine that's where your special relevance resides.

The first kind of relevance is inside-out. The second kind of relevance is outside-in. You may have a car or some other possession that is very relevant to you. It is agonizing to you if it gets smashed or stolen.

You have the same feelings if someone steals your love away from you. If it is taken away from you voluntarily, it's even worse.

We live by the meanings of our relationships to the people and the things in our lives. The more relevant the person or the possession is to you, the more mindshare the person or the possession has. If taken from us, we say we are broken-hearted. What we mean is that the loss of that mindshare is emotionally disruptive. It is our mind that is bereft.

We can fix that. It was our obsession in the first place. But when our relevance from the outside-in is disrupted, we can't fix it so easily. It was not our choice at the outset. It is not something we can control. If you "dump" someone, you can always find another. If someone "dumps" you, you cannot feel quite so optimistic. In the first case, it was your choice. In the second case, it was someone else's choice.

As you know—or at least have suspected—this is where most of your problems have their origin. If there is a discrepancy between how you see the world and how the world sees you, you have a problem.

As we have noted previously, if you are faced with this dilemma, you have three choices:

- Be fully in sync with the world, whatever it requires of you;

- By whatever means you can, put the world fully in sync with you; or

- Somewhere in between.

Most people don't want to adapt to others entirely. They want at least to feel that they are unique, special.

Most people are not capable of wooing the world to their aims in life. They may have tried and come up wanting.

Most people have their lives somewhere near the middle of this continuum. They are not fully in step with society. Nor are they fully autonomous. Most people find a comfortable mix somewhere near the middle. Most people

LEE THAYER

are still more determined by the culture that is their outer habitat than by their hopes and dreams.

As we saw two chapters back, most people are more likely to be outer determined than they are to be self determined.

The more you understand why this is so, the better your chances of not sharing the fate of most people.

Einstein was referring mainly to a "happy life" in the following comment. But it seems to me to apply to life in general:

> "If you want to live a happy life, tie it to a goal, not to people or objects."

In other words, being relevant to other people for some reason, or accumulating objects that are relevant to you, your relevance to yourself needs to come from your commitment to a goal. To escape the dilemma of trying to adapt fully to society, or trying to get people and things to adapt to you, measure your life in terms of progress toward your goals.

Your goals must be larger than you are. Don't devote your life either to the social world or to yourself. Get out of yourself and devote your life to your goals. That's how you become most relevant to yourself. It is as well how you become relevant to the world outside of yourself.

Being "Somebody"

If you are "somebody," you have relevance in the world outside yourself. If you are "nobody," then you don't.

To have an identity at all, you have to be someone to and for others. This means that you are in some way relevant to them. More importantly, it means that they are somehow relevant to you. Your mother had a heavy hand in making you somebody out of nobody.

Experiences that were impactful remain relevant to who you are. Your regrets, your concerns, your moments of joy are relevant to who you are.

Certain images—imaginary or photographic—are relevant to who you are. As you age, your memories are more relevant to you than are the events of yesterday or today. The people you have loved or hated, the possessions that you have especially treasured, remain relevant to who you are today. The ideas you have considered and the ideas you have opted to use become a part of who you are.

The British social observer and art critic John Ruskin (1819-1900) wrote as follows:

> *"What we think or what we know or what we believe is, in the end, of little consequence. The only thing of consequence is what we do."*

What is most relevant to us is what we did or didn't do, what was done to us or not. We are pleased by what we have done, or regretful. We anticipate what we are going to do. You have a private, inner life. But it is what you do about it in the world of people and things that creates or nurtures relevance. Leaders, like lovers, are relevant for what they do, not for their thoughts or intentions.

What you believe is certainly relevant to who you are. But what you *do* about your beliefs on your smaller or the larger stage is what has consequences—for you and for the social world you inhabit. You can know all kinds of stuff. But it is what you *do* with it that has consequences. You can have all kinds of strong feelings about another person or about the world you live in. But it is what you *do* about those feelings that has consequences.

You have your inner, private life. But it is what you do and what you permit to be done to you by that outer social and eventful world that constitutes relevance. You are relevant only if you matter *there*. You can gossip with your friends about your shared opinions. But that changes little in the real world.

If you want to do life as you would have it done, you have to perform it that way. All other people have to go on is your performance of who you are or who you would like to be. It is your performance in that world outside of you that has consequences.

In *A Woman of No Importance*, the incomparable satirist Oscar Wilde wrote,

> *"The secret of life is never to have an emotion that*
> *is unbecoming."*

If you want to "fit in," there is probably nothing more important. Have only the emotions that others have, and perform them only at the most appropriate time. Do life as others would have you do it.

From the same fertile author, we have this to ponder:

> *"Life is much to important a thing ever to talk seriously*
> *about it."*

Those who are familiar with Oscar Wilde's life and work are aware that he considered performing life far more important than talking about it. To him, talking about life is for those who are unlikely to *do* anything about their talk. It is how you perform life that has consequences, not what your wishes or your opinions might be.

Here's the catch (and the possibilities):

In order to be someone, it has to be in the eyes and the judgment of those in the world other than you. You can be someone by yourself only in the mirror. You can't be *someone* all by yourself—unless you want to be locked up or excommunicated.

Those others know you only by how you perform yourself. The world outside of yourself is a world of what happens, not an imaginary one. The consequences all flow from what is done, not what is hoped for or believed or valued.

As you perform yourself in your world, so shall you be. All it takes is one other to ratify your performance. That makes you someone on the local stage. To be someone on the larger stage requires lots and lots of people to ratify your performance.

And it is being relevant to some degree in that world outside yourself that makes you relevant to yourself.

Status and Hierarchy

When you were in school you experienced the fact that some of your fellow students were more important than others. Some were known to more people than others. They were the "popular" ones.

Some seemed to set the course and others seemed to follow. Some apparently had more power than others. Some seemed to set the fashions and others deferred to them—whether or not the fashions were in talk or dress or comportment.

There was a sort of hierarchy that determined who could say what to whom, who was inferior and who was superior, who was looked up to and who was looked down to. This is status—an apparently universal condition of that social world. There is a "pecking order." Even lion prides understand who eats first. There is always an alpha male or female. The rest are along to recognize that and defer.

Status is self-justifying and self-enforcing. People more often than not settle for their place in the social world. In one of his columns, our social observer and satirist Evan Esar offered the following (attributed to Carey Williams):

> *"You can tell the people who are in your class: they are the ones you hate to see get ahead of you."*

We may be envious of the people at the top. But it is those who are in our same "class" we watch carefully. We often see wrong in their even trying to get ahead. In Australia, this is referred to as the "tall poppy syndrome." If you see one of your peers trying to move up in the word, you do what you can to cut him or her down to the right size—yours.

If you have a certain status in society, you will be inclined to exhibit the symbols, the evidence, of having that status. And this can be your downfall. Esar wrote in another column:

> *"Some people own so many status symbols, they're absolutely in awe of themselves."*

Status is ephemeral and cannot be created or controlled except by a sort of marketing strategy. There are media personalities that got constructed on purpose. Their existence is still precarious. It comes down to that ineffable things we call status. We all know what it is. But it is not amenable to any one person's desires.

It is socially-constructed. It lives in talk and images and opinions. It emerges and is maintained largely by anonymous others. It has no tangible existence.

The British social philosopher and writer Alain Botton wrote as follows about this phenomenon and its grip on us in his book *Status Anxiety* (2004):

> *"If our position on the ladder is a matter of such concern,*
> *it is because our self-conception is so dependent upon*
> *what others make of us. Rare individuals aside . . . we rely*
> *on signs of respect from the world to feel tolerable to*
> *ourselves."*

"Signs of respect" could here be taken to mean what we are calling *relevance*—to others and thus to ourselves.

Botton continues, usefully to us in the present context:

> *". . . from failure will flow humiliation: a corroding*
> *that we have been unable to convince the world of*
> *our value and are henceforth condemned to consider*
> *the successful with bitterness and ourselves with*
> *shame."*

Some will, of course. Others in our culture might become fans, whether or not having failed to become celebrities or stars. The immense enthusiasm that fans often have for their celebrities might suggest that they are working off some envy. Performing as a fan becomes a substitute for performing as the celebrity status one has not achieved.

Status is positive for those who have it, often negative for those who don't. To have a life, you have to be *somebody*. And people have always been able to find that kind of alternative. Still, if your self-conception depends largely or entirely upon what others make of you, there is a downside to status.

In our culture, status is often connected with popular celebrity, with money, and thus with power. If you cannot garner these, you may be stuck with establishing your relevance in some other way. All of those other ways are of lesser status in our culture, of course.

The power part of status is intriguing. Ultimately, power can be defined thus:

> *You are more concerned with who you are than the more powerful person is concerned with who you are. It is the asymmetry that signals the power. What we consider to be the beautiful people are more powerful than what we consider to be the ugly people—unless ugly people have more money or a more unassailable position in society. Successful people are more powerful than those who are less successful.*

And so on. Even though we might pretend to embrace "equality," it seems to be human nature to settle into a hierarchy, into classes, into the have's and have-not's, those who have less or more than we do.

The British novelist William Golding was awarded a Nobel Prize mainly for his book, *Lord of the Flies*. A parable, the story is about a bunch of children marooned on a desert island. They make of their circumstances the need to have some sort of "society." So they create a hierarchy to make order out of chaos.

A hierarchy? Not the kind of society in which all are equal? Yes, a hierarchy—almost as if it were human nature.

But, then, hierarchy is ubiquitous in nature—especially among animals and insects. To the extent we evolved from nature, we would understand a hierarchy. Problems arise only when we try to substitute an egalitarian society for a class or hierarchical society. Most of today's most pressing social problems come from this attempted transition. Democracy can be the scourge of the earth when the society is in transition. Even in America, we do not practice democracy. We practice a kind of money, prestige, and celebrity hierarchy.

Almost always, as we practice what we call "love," one of the partners is dominant. We may trade off in this role. There is just no way to make a relationship or a transaction (or even a conversation) fully symmetrical.

My own Irish and German immigrant grandparents, who together operated a small self-sufficient farm in Kansas, were equal partners. They each had their chores. They valued one another not for which chores each owned, but for how well they did them. One set of chores was considered no more important than the other.

But when a decision had to be made, they did not vote. It was made by the one most qualified to do so. One was the absolute boss in the kitchen. One was the absolute boss of the fields and the horse-drawn equipment. They knew intuitively that a "vote" did not necessarily produce the best decision. They stepped up and deferred by tacit agreement. They were equals where the garden and the orchard were concerned. The whole—their survival and well-being—were more important to them than who was dominant.

The problem in the world we live in is not one of democracy vs. every other form of government. It is change. Wherever change occurs, expect perturbations, disagreements, even violence. People have nothing personal against the outside person involved in an affair. It is more often anxiety about the change that vexes them.

It is the same for you if you intend to make changes in your life. Somehow, you have to get through the turmoil for you and for others brought on by the changes you make.

Social Value

Who you are has to be of some value to your social world—else you will be less than "somebody." Your relevance to your outside world is measured by the social value you bring to it.

There is of course what you do and what you know. That will always vary in social value—or "social utility—and thus your relevance in that outer, social world.

As weird and irrational as it may seem at first, illness has more social value than health. People spend far more time sharing with others their illnesses than their good health. Bring good health into the conversation and the conversation goes flat. Bring a serious illness into the conversation, and it begins to heat up.

In that sense, illness is more contagious than health. Health does not befall us. Illness does. It raises the social relevance of the person who is suffering—just because of the way we talk about these two conditions. If there are new illnesses that no one in your circle has suffered, you would be a temporary celebrity to "have" it. If the illness itself is a media celebrity—cancer, for example—it will have followers. It may sound crazy. But all you have to do is look at the patterns. There are fashions in illness just as there are fashions in health.

If what you know has less value or utility to the social world than what others know, you will have less relevance than they have. If what you do in that social world has less value than what some others do, you will have less relevance than they have.

That's just the way our world works. If you would do life as you would have it, this is an important consideration. You can't have a life of *relevance* in the larger social world if what you know or what you do has little if any social value.

Fairness and Indifference

Nature is indifferent—in the sense of operating by its own logic, not that of people. We pretend not to be indifferent. For example, "fairness" is a purely human notion. It is an aspect of our human/social culture.

So children grow up with what's "fair" and what is not. This usually means that if something pleases or benefits them, it is fair. Otherwise it is not.

When they get old enough to vote, the notion of "fairness" becomes viral in politics and in everyday life.

The British writer and statesman G. K. Chesterton observed:

> *"The nearest thing that any honest man can come to the thing called impartiality is to confess that he is partial."*

We like to think that there are arenas where people can be impartial—as judges or scientists, for example—but most people put their own interests first. There are few rewards in life for being fair. But there are plenty of rewards for those who by perhaps unfair means pursue their own interests, indifferent to the cost to others.

If you choose a special friend among others, that is discrimination. Is that "fair"? If you choose a spouse and forego all others, one or more of whom might be better suited, is that fair, or just discriminatory? If people vote for a candidate because he or she is more attractive or stylish, is that fair? If we impose out ideologies on others, and kill them if they don't convert, is that fair? Sometimes good people die young and bad people live on. Is that fair?

Sometimes the world does not treat you as you would like to be treated. Is that fair? Your neighbor may have what you want but can't afford. Is that fair?

Some people have more problems than you have. Is that fair? Some people have fewer problems than you have. Is that fair?

Fairness may be a good thing. But we can't remake the world to accommodate everyone's personal interests. The natural and social worlds you live in are largely indifferent to your needs and your hopes and dreams. That may not be *fair*. But that's the way things are.

If you would do life as you would have it done, you may be treated indifferently rather than what you would consider to be fairly. Indifference is akin to randomness. Things happen over which neither you nor anyone else has control. Is the world to be faulted for its own workings, its own impenetrable logic?

The randomness of events may always arise to thwart your interests. As the columnist Evan Esar once wrote:

> *"Life is an endless series of bounces, some as predictable as the rebound of a basketball, others as unpredictable as the rebound of a football."*

What is unpredictable cannot be prevented. What is unpredictable cannot be controlled. Life in the world outside of you is that way more often than not. You can't be certain how the ball is going to bounce. You have to play the bouncing ball regardless. Forget fairness. Get with reality.

Relevance is determined by the outside world. Learning how to be "fair" with yourself can be useful. Trying to extract fairness from the randomness of the world is not.

Johnny Carson once remarked,

> *"If life were fair, Elvis would be alive and all the impersonators would be dead."*

The solution? Be the random event that has its way with the world of randomness.

That would be *doing* life rather than commiserating about it. *Your relevance to the world and thus to yourself lies **there***, in action rather than complaint.

XIX

. . . Doing and Undoing Life

"Life consists of what a [person] is thinking of all day."

—Ralph Waldo Emerson

"Life is the only game in which the object of the game is to learn the rules."

—Ashleigh Brilliant

"You are a victim of the rules you live by."

—Jenny Holzer

People have always been able to make a life for themselves out of some combination . . .

- Of who they already are. We *evolve* out of who we are, not who we aspire to be;
- Of what is necessary and possible in their inner and outer habitats; and
- Of the fortuitous events that occur along the way which bear upon their lives in some way.

People can never start with a clean slate. We are always at any moment who we *are* at that moment. You may wish to be someone else. But you have to start from where you are and who you are. The first claim on your future life is the life you already have.

Who you are at any time makes certain things necessary, and other things possible. Combine that with the world outside of you and you have another set of necessities and possibilities. How you "read" the facts of the matter bears upon what you can do about them.

Things happen. You may permit those happenings to change your feelings about yourself and how you go about architecting your life. Some things bear upon your life almost irresistibly. Other events that occur can change your life only because you permit them to do so.

You can't do much about where and when you were born, or who you were born to. Those people and that place were the first and lasting influences on your life. People come into and go out of your life in ways you cannot control. All attachments to other people as you go along will be serendipitous—inexplicable, seemingly random. But they will influence the trajectory of your life in powerful ways. You must choose those people for your purposes, not for theirs. If you have a guiding purpose in life, this will tell you who you should allow to influence you, and who you should not.

This is especially the case for the media you consume. If the media fare you consume contributes to what you want to be when you grow up, it can be a positive influence. If it doesn't, it will be either clutter (an impediment) or a powerful deterrent.

Everyone has a life of some sort. It is well to remember this. The life they have may be purely adventitious. They were made by those inner and outer influences that just happened, with no real purpose of their own. If so, do not emulate them. If you do, you will be buffeted by whatever way the wind blows.

If you aim to avoid being "mediocre," you have to resist mediocrity. You will be surrounded by its influences. Having a life of no particular worth is easy. Its influences function like gravity. You are not always aware of those influences. But they occur.

In this book, you may have gotten the impression that any way of life is equal to any other way of life—that if you just tinker with it a little bit like a dilettante, you are doing life as you would have it done. That is not how you should think about it.

If you are not aiming for the *ideal*, your efforts will produce a different way of life that is essentially the same as what you had. Pop psych recipes will guarantee that you will just be exchanging one fashion for another. There are different ways of being average or mediocre. Pick your poison. To be endorsed by others is just that—endorsement by others. They will bring you down to what are the common denominators in that group.

The only aim that is not commonly held is the *ideal*. The only life worth struggling to achieve is the ideal life.

This means you have to think for yourself. You have to open yourself to the influence of those who have had as *their* aim in life-making only the ideal. Mark Twain said:

> "Be good and you will be lonesome."

If you want to live comfortably and be "well-liked" by lots of people, you have to be like those people are. If you surround yourself by influences other than the ideal, you will become whatever those influences make necessary. To pursue the ideal means that you will not fit in very well. If you succeed, you will be lonesome. Unless, of course, your mentors are those who know what it means to pursue the ideal, and how that is the only life worth having.

So it is not so much a matter of doing life as *you* would have it done, but of doing life as it *should* be done.

You need the strength to do this. That strength, Leonardo da Vinci believed,

> "... is born of constraint and dies in freedom."

There will be plenty of constraints. Others will want you to be like they are. That would mainly be who they are—nothing truly purposeful, just settling for what has come their way. Their influence may be mostly tacit.

But it will be powerful. You need to be more powerfully committed to the ideal to be able to break free of those constraints.

It's far easier to be whatever you have become than to pursue the ideal. That's a constraint as well. Let your strength be born of that. Freedom and the comfort that comes from letting the world make your life are your enemies, as we have seen.

Benjamin Franklin was one of those rare individuals who sought the ideal in all aspects of his life. He had an uncanny knack for seeing what his outer obstacles were in making his life as it ought to be. He wrote:

> *"So convenient a thing it is to be a reasonable creature,*
> *since it enables one to find or make a reason for everything*
> *one had a mind to do."*

In other words, most people can *rationalize* their thoughts and actions before, during, and after they occur. This is a kind of inner nemesis that gets people off the hook for the consequences of their thoughts and actions. If you excuse yourself, you will be unable to see what part of the problem you are. And that's the most important thing to know.

If you intend to do life as it should be done, you need to clean up your own act first. You need to see yourself in the context of whatever relevance you have in that outer world. You need to see it as it is (as far as possible), and that requires seeing yourself as you are (as far as that is possible).

People can indeed find or make up a reason for everything they have done or may be planning to do. The question is: will that reason serve your long range purposes?

This observation by Aristotle (384-322 B.C.) may be helpful:

> *"We must enjoin everyone that has the power to live*
> *according to his own choice to set up for himself some*
> *object for the good life to aim at . . . , with reference to*
> *which he will then do all his acts, since not to have*
> *one's life organized in view of some end is a mark of*
> *much folly."*

LEE THAYER

It may be "folly" from an observer's standpoint. But it is insidious for the person, who will then see life not in his or her own lights but as being victimized by whatever can be rationalized to be the culprit. This will certainly not be oneself. But it is not so much folly that you will suffer. It is the failure to do life as it should be done—a sort of creeping suicide.

To organize one's life in view of some worthy cause or purpose for living is thus the point. The problem is that if people have the power to live according to their own choice, they may abdicate the responsibility. They may fritter away their lives, having no guiding purpose for doing life. They may deny responsibility for the consequences of their choices. This is not so much folly as it is self-destruction.

You cannot do life as it should be done unless you take responsibility for doing so. It matters little what your thoughts or intentions are. The only thing that really matters is not that you thought to do it, or that you understood how to do it, but that you *did* it. Life is in the doing, not the contemplating or explaining.

To be inspired to do life in this way or that is not the same thing as doing life as it should be done. The only justification is how you did life, not how you rationalized it.

More has been written or said about doing life than perhaps any other subject. Of advice, we have a surfeit. Of the results of that advice, we have little to show. People today seem to have more disillusionment about their lives than people did centuries back.

For the most part, life is episodic. First something happens, and then something else. We chase here or there out of what we consider to be necessity. But living life as they should never seems to become a real necessity for most people.

We defer life in order to get through the day.

Balzac, the famous French novelist (there were ninety of them!) made many observations on the human condition. One pertinent to our path here is as follows:

> *"Life is simply what our feelings do to us."*

If you can manage to have the feelings that do to you what you need in order to do life as it should be done, then you are off and running. But we think of our feelings as something that just happen to us. If that is what you believe, then life will be something that just sort of happens to you.

The point to recall here is that everything is subject to your interpretation of it. The outer world is full of obligations and social rules and protocols. But your mind is free to interpret according to your own ends, as Aristotle said, and as Eleanor Roosevelt echoed when she suggested that no one can make you feel bad without your permission.

Within broad limits, you can choose your feelings. They are yours. Manage them as you might any other endeavor. They will certainly bear upon your life, as Balzac observed. But which ones? That's up to you. And how? That's up to you. That is your prerogative. Exercise it.

The story of your life looking back is one that you create. There were happenings that stand out as being important. But those happenings need to be connected by a story line that is plausible and provides you with a sense of your ongoing continuity—who you *are* in your world.

The story of your life looking forward is the same. Things will occur in your life. There will be beginnings and endings. The story of your life is how you connect the dots. You can write it. Or you can allow it to be written for you. This is ultimately your choice. Not a easy one. But nothing worthwhile is easy.

The German parodist Christian Morgenstern may have put it in the severest way:

> *"If you do not want to conquer the world every single day,*
> *you will lose more of it day by day."*

This may require some thought. Conquering the world may be a matter of making you the perpetrator and the world the victim, rather than the other way around.

Most important, however, is the idea that how you do life today predicts to how you *can* do life tomorrow. Life is cumulative. What you don't accomplish today in terms of doing life as it should be done makes it less likely to be possible tomorrow. And so on, until the possibilities all but evaporate.

Starting next week is already too unlikely.

The German journalist Kurt Tucholsky, who escaped treason at the hands of the Nazis wrote:

"Expect nothing. Today: that is your life."

It is the life that has evolved from the way you have done it up to today. If you would do life differently, there is only today to take the second step.

You undo life when you do not do life as you should be doing it.

"Success" and Failure

You may "succeed" or not in your own estimation, or that of your mother or your lover. Success is defined in many ways. The way that makes the most difference is what success means in the outer, social world.

Your relevance is out there, in that world.

There, you will have your ups and downs. There is no smooth ride where people's opinions are concerned. You may be "in" one day and "out" the next. You may or may not have your "fifteen minutes" in the limelight.

There is only one kind of success that is independent of the others' judgments. That is success in the pursuit of your own good and worthy goals in life. Success in that outer world turns on the fashions of the day—including the fashions of defining success. If you depend upon relevance there to measure relevance to yourself, you will live precariously.

The only way to avoid the fickleness of others' approbation is to mind your own business. And your own business is that of learning how to do life as it should be done.

If you have no purpose in life, then it seems you cannot fail. But that is the failure that most mutilates your life. Just because you are well-liked does not mean you are on the right path. Just because you are in your comfort zone does not mean that you are on the right path.

If you define yourself, you might indeed fail. But that may not be your failure. It may be society's failure.

Doing life as it should be done is not for social prostitutes. There is nothing that is more courageous. There is nothing that is more life-giving. To have a right life requires you to make it.

If you want to be a celebrity, you will end up having to suck up to your fans. That is not life-making. That is life-spending.

As our first great novelist Miguel de Cervantes (*Don Quixote*) said,

> *"Show me who thou art with, and I will tell thee what thou art."*

Your "parents," the philosopher E. M. Cioran intimated, need to be those who know how to make life as it should be because they have done it that way. These need to be your mentors—those who can make it possible for you, and necessary.

The quote from Cervantes is perhaps blindingly obvious. You will become like those you hang out with. If they haven't a clue, you won't have a clue. Tap the richest resources for how to think, how to be, and how to do.

Success in our culture is primarily a matter of becoming wealthy. But, as Nietzsche quipped, success has always been a big liar. Money does not guarantee success in life, as many financially well-off people have demonstrated in modern times.

And far too many people consider themselves failures because they don't have lots of money. You don't need lots of money to make a life worth living. What you need is a good and worthy purpose, and the diligence to work at it until you die.

Success seems to consist of being envied by people who would like to be successful. This returns us to an earlier provocation: "Reality is a shared hallucination." Money isn't real. Experiences are. People who experience loving and being loved because they have learned what it takes are richer by far than people who have no more than money to show for having lived a pecuniary life.

People who equip themselves to have the most extraordinary personal experiences have succeeded far beyond those who are merely envied. People who devote themselves to becoming exceptionally competent at what they do are as a result happier in life, have better health, and live longer. That must be some kind of "success." Cultures and other people may define success by what is easily countable. They could be wrong.

More is not success. Living is. Doing life as it should be done is its own reward. Incentives do not tempt people who have a good and worthy purpose in life.

In his "The Fallacy of Success" (1908), Lord Chesterton remarked:

> *"There are only two ways . . . of succeeding. One is by doing*
> *very good work, the other is by cheating."*

Those of us who have survived the early years of the 21st century are immersed in stories about success by cheating. If cheating is the road to success, we should all seek to fail.

The famous capitalist Malcolm S. Forbes, in his reflection "Arrived," wrote intriguingly:

> *"By the time*
> *we make it*
> *we've had it."*

The endless pursuit of money, like the endless pursuit of fame, is as exhausting as it is intoxicating. It depletes the soul—which you need much of if you are to undertake doing life as it should be done. Like every addiction, it ruins the person and is a burden on society.

In his *Note Book,* published posthumously in 1927, our homespun philosopher Elbert Hubbard put it succinctly:

"There is no such thing as success in a bad business."

To call people successful who further their own interests in a bad business is deceptive labeling. They have already failed the rest of us, no matter what they have accumulated for themselves.

There are penalties for what we call "success" in a bad business, a culture that rewards the wrong things. In the *Daily Express* in 1956, Nancy Astor was quoted as saying:

"The penalty of success is to be bored by people who used to snub you."

In our culture, we look up to people who seem to have more public relevance than we have. We look down on people who seem to have less public relevance than we have. That "public relevance" comes primarily from the media. Or it comes from one's status. The CEO is more closely watched and more talked about than others in an organization. In your community and your occupation, some people are more talked about than others. That's status or degree of relevance and it is often considered a form of success.

Why successful people are "boring" is that they didn't get to be "successful" because they were interesting or thoughtful. They got there because they were looked up to by other people. The expression, "Nothing breeds success like success" suggests that if you are successful in the eyes of others, this will serve to make you even more successful.

Your identity depends in large part on what others think of you. If people in large numbers consider you to be "successful," you may be stuck with their perspective.

You have to ignore this phenomenon because it would be rare that others' adulation or deference would in any way further your aim to be doing life as it should be done. That requires you to choose as auditors those who have demonstrated that they can do life as it should be done. That's a small group, immune to the popular ideas about "success."

Socrates was one of those. But consider what happened to him. He was ordered to give up his principles if he wanted to live. He chose to die rather than join a corrupted society. Gandhi risked his life daily, as did Sister Teresa. You may not have to risk that much. But if you abide by the fashions of the day, you will have to put most of your efforts into changing your beliefs when the fashions change.

As the famous playwright Bertolt Brecht once remarked,

> *"Because things are the way they are, things will not stay the way they are."*

Because things are the way they are because they got to be that way, they could certainly become some other way. Doing life as it should be done is relatively immune to the fickleness of things—or of people.

Social life is replete with hypocrisy. Who you end up being probably depends most on which lies you buy into. In other words, how dupable you may be. If you don't have a guiding purpose in life, you are susceptible to being seduced by whatever (or whoever) comes along.

Choosing to do life as it should be done makes you impervious to casual hypocrisy. The only antidote to being suckered in by the hypocrisies of others or of the larger world is to refuse to be a hypocrite yourself. Doing life as it *should* be done provides you with the immunity you need in a hypocritical world. Knowing that the easiest person to deceive is yourself, you must know yourself so well and focus so clearly on your purpose that it is impossible to be hypocritical about your life.

Don't wish. This makes you dupable. *Do.* That leaves no space for deceit.

Props and Prostheses

- Choose the props that further your purpose in life. The ones you don't need will be a way that others might use to manipulate you.
- Anything that extends your vision or your strength is a prosthetic.

Never be identified by your prostheses. The more tools or toys you seem to need will cause others to discount your commitment or your strength to carry out your will. Don't give the world that advantage.

The Poetics and Politics of Life

To live well and rightly—for you and the world around you—is an art. It requires the perspective and the machinations of an artist.

You cannot do life as it should be done by rational means. You have to imagine who you could or should be. Then you have to have the tools and techniques to realize in your world what you have imagined.

Because you are unique (or aim to be), there is no recipe for doing this. You have to *invent* the tools and techniques you need. You must be the poet of the story of your life. This cannot be done by a group. It has to be done by you, using the other people in your life as a supporting cast. For them to support you, you must support them. This is what poets do with words, and what you must do with words and deeds.

The antithesis of art is politics. Even though the art world is, like every other human domain, highly politicized, the artist cannot do his or her work as a politician. You may fail. But you must fail on your own terms, not those of a hypocritical world.

As Ralph Waldo Emerson said,

> *"Insist on yourself; never imitate."*

That doesn't mean be who you *are*, which so many take to be the case these days. It means become who you *should* be and you will become one of a kind. You can't become who you *should* by imitating others. You have to be the artist of your own life and put it out there for the benefit or the disparagement of others.

And, as Emerson wrote elsewhere:

> *"The reward of a thing well done is to have done it."*

The reward for doing life as it should be done is to have done it.

The 19th-century British writer Samuel Butler might have been echoing Aristotle when he wrote:

"Don't learn to do, but learn in doing."

The poet's life is one of learning how to do poetry. The artist's life is how to learn to do art. Your life is how to learn to do your life as it should be done. Knowing how to do it is like an unfertilized egg. The only way to learn how to do life as it should be done is to do it that way in order to learn how.

Everyday life is mostly political in nature. Each is after his or her private gain, but disguises this in the rhetoric that would make it appear to be for others' benefit. Most contemporary marketing is like that. Entreaties of love and of loyalty are often like that—having your way under the guise of benefiting others. We are afloat and aimless in a world politicized in this sense.

Doing life as it should be done is a-political. Tending to your business (doing your life as it should be done) may force others around you to do the same. There may be material rewards for playing the political game, in gossip next door or at the national level. But it shrivels the soul—which, again, is what you need to develop in order to do life as it should be done.

If your life is not a work of art, with you the artist, what will it be?

Life-Making

About the interminable problems of life, we are deluged by metaphors and recipes. Much of literature, of expertise, sermons, and folklore are devoted to explaining our problems to us and offering (for some price) the solutions to those problems.

But solutions beget problems. And the world that swirls around you is one that identifies or creates ever-new problems in order to profit from solutions to those problems. Many friendships ensue from sharing the same problems.

"Life" is big business. Turn on the TV at anytime of the day or night. You will be exposed to stories about life gone wrong, or of recipes about how to make it go right. There are endless explanations about lives gone wrong. There are endless recipes about how to make your life go right. If you have this or that symptom, there is a cure for it. All you have to do is believe it and buy it.

But solutions beget more problems. The supply for those who profit from revealing your problems and the solutions to them is endless.

As popular and ubiquitous as it is, that is no way of doing life. The medical industry, for example, knows that there is no better healer for what ails you than your own body. But that industry cannot survive and grow unless it can find a problem for which it has the solution, for which someone has to pay. It is an industry that is not fixable because it is utterly consistent with our cultural predilections.

Going back to the provocations at the head of this chapter: If life is the only game in which the object of the game is to learn the rules (Brilliant), and yet if you are a victim of the rules you live by (Holzer), what's the point?

One metaphor for life, which may have more staying power than most, was provided by the same Samuel Butler as above. He wrote:

> "We are like billiard balls in a game played by unskillful
> players, continually being nearly sent into a pocket, but
> hardly ever getting right into one, except by a fluke."

We live "stochastically"—meaning one darn thing after another, a chain of more or less random happenings out of which we concoct a story of our lives that makes sense to us. We bounce from one thing into another. Once in a while, we get lucky—accidentally ending up in the right "pocket." We get lucky and happiness befalls us. We get unlucky and misery befalls us. We ricochet like billiard balls because other forces are wielding the cue.

No matter. People at all times and places have made their lives out of the exigencies of their circumstances, the customs of their tribe, and out of the creative powers of their imaginations.

In their book, *Autumn: A Spiritual Biography of the Season*, Gary Schmidt and Susan Falch wrote:

> "... our lives are made not to run in smooth and easy paths ...
> Our lives are messy, sometimes scheduled, sometimes
> random, sometimes prepared for, sometimes taken on the
> fly as we juggle our own blazing experiences, all of which
> come at us with their own joys and sorrows ... beginnings
> and endings are part of our experiences ... [reminding] us
> that we are maybe not our own; we neither mark out nor
> control all the paths we may take."

You still won't control all of those happenings and exigencies of the outside world. But you *can* control your interpretations of those exigencies, or of the customs of your tribe. But you *can* set a course for *learning* how to do life as it should be done and stay that path, making any off-course corrections you need to make whenever they occur.

In his autobiography, James Michener wrote:

> "The master in the art of living ... simply pursues his
> vision of excellence at whatever he does, leaving
> others to decide whether he is working or playing."

The more a master in the art of living he or she becomes, they will always be doing both. The master makes no distinction.

A life lived in total subjugation to the events or to the customs of the tribe is a life half-lived. So is a life lived in direct pursuit of one's immediate wants and desires a life half-lived. What you want is a life fully lived. You can achieve that only by pursuing a good and worthy purpose, and minding your own business—which that now is.

If most people have a choice, they'll take it (to paraphrase Yogi Berra). The master stays the course he or she has set.

People's lives are incoherent, mostly irrational. Our explanations of them are not. If you would do life as it should be done, you will explain your life only in a way that furthers your cause.

The Nobel laureate poet and essayist Milan Kundera asks if that is not indeed the definition of *biography*: *"An artificial logic imposed on an incoherent succession of images."*

One thing is certain: Life is a performing art. And you perform your life according to what it means to you and what you want to mean to people. You can learn how to manage both. In that sense, you are the author and the architect of your life.

One other thing is fairly certain. It is that if you don't do your life as you should, the world will make of you whatever it will.

The eminent psychologist Mihaly Csikszentmihalyi said, in a dialogue about "happiness":

> *"The quality of life does not depend on happiness alone, but also on what one does to be happy. If one fails to develop goals that give meaning to one's existence, if one does not use the mind to its fullest, then good feelings fulfill just a fraction of the potential we possess. True happiness involves the pursuit of worthy goals. Without dreams, without risks, only a trivial semblance of living can be achieved."*

It was once thought to be the original sin to fail to make of one's raw material all that could be made of it. Doing life as it should be done may be the ultimate responsibility we humans have inherited.

David Dunning said that

> *"Ignorance profoundly channels the course we take in life."*

At least now you would not want to claim *that* excuse.

The counterpoint comes from the English journalist William Hazlitt:

> *"Even in knowledge there should be always something left to know in order to arouse curiosity and excite hope."*

May this pragmatic probe do just that for you.

AFTERWORD

Life is, until it ends, a work in progress. Life goes on, through all of its twists and turns, ups and downs. It's not over until it is over.

So are our explanations of life. They, too, are always a work in progress. They will not cease until there is no one to write a further poem, a further aphorism, a further book, a further film or story, or to undertake a further work of art.

Your life is a work in progress. If you had it to do over again, you might make some course corrections. You might not. In any event, if you were to read this book again, it would seem different to you. Different points would attract your attention. Life is like that. When what you once anticipated or expected is now in the past, it will not seem to you what it did at the outset.

You can't repeat any moment of your life as it was. You have changed as a result of it.

It is the same with this book. Once you have thought about it, once you have digested it and do with it what you will, you will have changed.

The purpose of the book is to aid your thinking about these vital ideas, to help you digest them and do with them what you will. If you think about what struck you as most important and do something about it, you will have changed.

My intent is that these changes will be for the better—for you, and for all of those around you.

If you change, the world changes. If you change for the better, the world changes for the better.

Doing life is not a hobby. It's the real thing. It's the only thing. Here are some pragmatic ideas about how to do your only thing better than you might otherwise have done it.

This book gives you a place to stand. You need a solid place to stand in order to reach a better place. That's why you have this book.

The life you have derives from how it is explained to you, how you explain it to yourself, and how you explain everything that happens in it. The life you can have depends upon how you explain it—upon how you *can* explain it.

Your life begins with an explanation and ends with an explanation. In between, you will live out your life according to how you explain it. Explain it well, and your life will be well. Explain it poorly and your life will fulfill your explanations of it.

That's what the "Pragmatist" means. The more you know about the realities of life, the more able you will be to remodel yourself in the context of the real world.

It will never be perfect, the life you live. That's because perfectionism is a disease, not a method. You have to do the best you can with what you have to do it with.

Doing life will always be a work in progress. It's like learning how to play the violin after the concert has begun. If you ever stop learning how to play the game of life, you have forfeited.

Don't.

ABOUT THE BOOK AND THE AUTHOR

Dr. Thayer's study of the human condition has been both extensive and intensive. He has presented his perspectives before his peers and scholars around the world, and in the 28 books he has authored or edited. His research into the human condition began more than a half-century ago.

The study of "the human condition" is intensely multidisciplinary – ranging from biology and genetics to sociology and anthropology and literature. The human condition is always a product of human cultures. Fundamental beliefs vary. And we are always some amalgam of our beliefs and our imaginations, and of the raw stuff and the social stuff of which we are made.

People live the stories they believe themselves to be in. It is the trajectory of a person's life that matters to that person. The present is empirically where the person's imagined past and his or her imagined future are protagonists in the playing out of behavior in the present – thus the idea of "doing life." We don't actually *have* a life that is fixed and immutable. It is always a work in progress. We *do life* according to who we are at any moment, which is a result of the myriad choices we have made in the past.

Our hopes and dreams give lie to the picture we have of ourselves. That picture could be imagined to be different. If an artist does not like what he or she has painted, it can be painted over. If a person does not like who he or she is, there is no starting over. "Doing life" is painting over the life one already has but is dissatisfied with. Every starting point is who one is at that moment.

In this book, Lee Thayer brings to bear his formidable intellectual resources from his years of research to take his readers into the pragmatics of doing life. Painting over one's present portrait is more difficult than starting from scratch. But there is no possibility of starting from scratch.

Just as the serious scholar has to build on what he already knows, the serious student of life – that's you, the reader – has to make any future life out of the material available for doing so. That's what "doing life" pragmatically is all about.

Pragmatic means practicable. The author has always been guided by the practicability of his insights. His journey has always been illuminated by what could be done with this or that idea.

In this book, he wants to share with you not just some ideas, but what you might be able to do with them in your life. "Doing life" is about having the kind of life you *do* – or *could* do. You have the life you have by doing it the way you do.

Here's a book that enables you to choose and what to do about it, from an author who knows what you are up against. It is your understanding of what you are up against that best informs your decision, whatever that may be.

The best authors are the best therapists. There is no one better at this than Lee Thayer.

If this doesn't do it for you, or if you want more insight, try one or more of the author's books, such as:

- *Communication! A Radically New Approach to Life's Most Perplexing Problem*
- *On Communication*
- *Pieces: Toward a Revisioning of Life*
- *Explaining Things: Inventing Ourselves and Our Worlds*

[…available from the publisher, Xlibris, from Barnes & Noble or your local bookstore, or from Amazon.com]

CPSIA information can be obtained at www.ICGtesting.com
Printed in the USA
LVOW11s1424181114

414327LV00001B/52/P

9 781469 163437